OUTRAGEOUS

OUTRAGEOUS

A Contemporary View of U. S. Puerto Rican Relations

Brian Irving
Eastern New Mexico University - Roswell

ABOUT THE BOOK

Puerto Rico became a colony of the United States in December of 1898, it is still a colony over 100 years later. In December of 1998, a status plebiscite was held in which the voters of the island were asked to vote for their status preference. Four alternatives were offered, they included statehood, commonwealth, independence or free association. More than 50% of the voters selected the fifth column which was "none of the above." The author discusses all aspects of current U.S. Puerto Rican relations and suggests a solution for the endless debate about the future of the island.

Dedicated to my Colleagues
at
Eastern New Mexico University

CONTENTS

Preface   xi

Introduction   xv

1. Historical Perspective   1

2. University Level Funding   6

3. Sports   12

4. Language   16

5. Nutritional Assistance   23

6. Section 936   26

7. Runaway Plants   31

8. Commonwealth   36

9. Nationalism   39

10. Status Debate   46

11. Historical Accidents   52

12. The Escape Valve   57

13. The Problem of Governing   62

14. Plebiscite   67

15. Conclusion   71

16. Footnotes   79

PREFACE

Since I retired from teaching at the Inter American University of Puerto Rico in 1981, I have lived on the island for part of the year and on the mainland during the summers. While in Puerto Rico, particularly since the beginning of the campaign to the now discredited plebiscite of 1993, the media on the island, particularly the newspapers are filled daily with articles, stories, editorials and interviews with everybody and anybody about the status of Puerto Rico. There is no way to avoid it, and of course meetings, rallies, parades and visits of congressional leaders from the mainland add to the general frenzy. This is, of course, becoming more and more overpowering as the 1998 plebiscite gets nearer. While on the island, it is hard to believe that people anywhere, and particularly in the United States, are interested in talking about anything else.

And yet every May, as I return to the mainland, usually spending a week or two in New York and Washington, before returning to Wisconsin, it is as if Puerto Rico, not to mention its status, did not exist. I have friends in New York and Washington who regularly send me articles about Puerto Rico, but only once or twice a year does the <u>New York Times</u> even mention the island; <u>The Washington Post</u> does somewhat better, but in neither paper do they discuss the issue of status. When friends in the States ask me about Puerto Rico, there will often be such questions as: "It's a colony, isn't it, like Hawaii used to be?" or "Someone told me they were going to make it a state. Is that true? Don't they all speak Spanish?"

Occasionally close friends or relatives will ask me serious questions about Puerto Rico, its history and its economy, but they are so completely ignorant about the island that I don't know how to begin explaining its problems. They do know that almost all Puerto Ricans are devout Catholics and either work on large sugar plantations or have their own little farms where they raise whatever it is you raise to make your own tortillas. When I explain that when I first went to the island in 1951 there was not a single Puerto Rican priest there, that most of them had to be sent down from Boston, and that the majority of Puerto Ricans work in factories, live in cities, receive tax breaks and that their daily diet of rice and beans has to be imported, they don't listen. They know better than that. They are reassured when I explain that many still have chickens in their back yards. If I start to explain the parking problems around the malls, which are taking business away from the downtown sections or pass on the statistic that there are more automobiles per mile of paved road than anywhere else in the world, they stare at me with disbelief. But they do accept my word that there are 1,319 people per square mile. No wonder they all want to move to New York, Chicago and Florida! Why do we let them in?

Prof. Irving has attempted to explain the dilemma of Puerto Rico at the crossroads. Puerto Rico has been a colony of the United States for one hundred years and it is important that mainlanders and particularly their elected leaders understand this dilemma and help to resolve the status questions. Prof. Irving is uniquely qualified to write this story having lived and worked on the island for 27 years. He worked during the majority of those years at the Inter American University of Puerto Rico as a faculty member and as an administrator at four different locations, he even taught Puerto Rican history in Spanish.

Let us hope that some of the information contained in this book will help the congress in their deliberations.

Dr. James Cooper

INTRODUCTION

The word outrageous has been used as the title of this book, to describe the present relationship between Puerto Rico and the United States. It was originally used in this context by the former senator of Arkansas, David Pryor, to describe Section 936 of the Internal Revenue Code which has allowed many companies to avoid paying federal taxes on profits made in Puerto Rico. Also outrageous in Senator Pryor's estimation is the fact that the same companies (mostly pharmaceutical companies) which make enormous untaxed profits, continue to sell their drugs to mainland taxpayers at "outrageous" prices.

The purpose of this study is to help shed some light on the Puerto Rican status debate which has been waged for a hundred years. It began when American troops landed at Gúanica Bay on July 25, 1898, and continues today. In November of 1993, a plebiscite was held with the aim of finally resolving the debate. The results of that plebiscite, however, were inconclusive, because there was no clear majority winner. The results were as follows:

Pro-Statehood voters polled 46.2% of the vote.

Pro-Commonwealth forces polled 48.4% of the vote.

Supporters of the Independence option garnered 4.4% if the total

The Commonwealth Party claimed victory and have since been advocating an "enhanced commonwealth", which translates into more autonomy and more federal funds.

The Committee on Resources and the committee on International Relations of the U.S. House of Representatives have since gone on record to the effect that "it is incontrovertible that Puerto Rico's present status is that of an unincorporated territory subject in all respects to the authority of the U.S. Constitution, in other words it is a colony, and as such, the current status does not provide guaranteed citizenship to the inhabitants of the territory of Puerto Rico, nor does the current status provide the basis for recognition of a separate Puerto Rican sovereignty or a binding government-to-government status pact."1/

The plebiscite of November 14, 1993, not only was inconclusive as to its results, but some of the options chosen by the political parties as part of their status options are not feasible, according to the congress. An example of this is the idea of a combined Puerto Rican and U.S. citizenship, or dual citizenship, put forth by the Independence Party of Puerto Rico. The committees involved with the status of Puerto Rico described that option as "misleading and inconsistent with the fundamental principles of separate nationality and non-interference by two sovereign countries in each other's internal affairs, which includes the regulation of citizenship."2/

Certain parts of the commonwealth option, including a permanent union with the United States and guaranteed U.S. citizenship were deemed not possible 3/, because one congress cannot tie the hands of a future congress. What is needed is for the "congress to define the real options for change and the true legal and political nature of the status quo, so that the people can know what the actual choices will be in the future."4/

The latter ends with a sentence which reads: "the question of Puerto Rico's political status remains open and unresolved."5/ At the present time the Congress is trying to determine exactly what options will be acceptable, the plan is for a new plebiscite to be held in 1998, which will allow the Puerto Rican people to make a decision on their real options. If, however, the results of the plebiscite in 1998, are inconclusive then there will be future plebiscites until one of the options wins and is approved by the congress.

According to the congress the only options are: "1) separate sovereignty and full national independence; 2) separate sovereignty in free association with the United States; 3) full integration into the United States political system ending unincorporated status and leading to statehood."6/

Since the plebiscite of 1993, elections were held in Puerto Rico in November of 1996, and the leader of the Statehood Party, Pedro Rosselló received 51.2% of the vote: Hector Luis Acevedo, of the Commonwealth Party received 44.4%; and David Noriega Rodriguez of the Independence party received 3.8% of the vote.7/

The Statehood party also elected its Resident Commissioner in Washington; maintained their majority in the senate and house of representatives and won two thirds of the 78 mayoral elections on the island.8/ Governor Pedro Rosselló was the first candidate for governor who ever received more that a million votes in a Puerto Rican election.9/ This victory was all the more astonishing, because Pedro Rosselló had lost several other votes where he had put his prestige on the line, including the plebiscite of 1993.

In the analysis of the election, David Noriega Rodriguez, the candidate for governor for the Independence party claimed that the elections of November 5, 1996 were not a referendum on the status of Puerto Rico. 10/ The surveys conducted by the experts seem to support the view of Noriega, because the voters put the political status way down the list of political priorities. What the voters wanted was for Pedro Rosselló to complete or continue his program for the island. 11/

Since the elections of November, 1992, the United Stated congress has emphasized a balanced budget and has even forced President Clinton to at last pay lip service to that goal. This emphasis has certainly brought the growing cost of Puerto Rico under scrutiny. Since 1970, "Some 90 billion dollars in federal funds have poured into the island according to the U.S. Census Bureau and Planning Board figures."12/ This does not include the 3 billion dollars which U.S. companies don't contribute to the federal treasury every year.

This new attention has also focused on the fact that the cost of Puerto Rico continues to increase year after year; and "the longer Puerto Rico remains a colony, the longer that U.S. taxpayers are going to support a dole economy."13/ According to Robert Friedman federal funds to Puerto Rico "keep pouring in and now have reached more that $10 billion annually."

The United States acquired Puerto Rico as a result of her victory over Spain in 1898, military and strategic reasons were paramount in this decision. The idea was that Puerto Rico would serve as a military base to protect the projected canal across Central America, in particular, the United States wanted to control the Mona Passage between Puerto Rico and the Dominican Republic, because the Mona Passage constitutes a major shipping lane between the Atlantic Ocean and the Caribbean Sea.

After Puerto Rico was acquired from Spain, in December of 1898, Puerto Rico was treated as a typical colony until the 1930's. The purpose was to benefit business interests in the United States, in particular the sugar companies, nevertheless, there was some progress toward self government, and with the passage of the Jones Act in 1917, Puerto Ricans became United States Citizens.

The Great Depression was a disaster for the island, but after the election of President Franklin Roosevelt in 1932, New Deal programs were introduced into Puerto Rico. The first of these was founded in 1933, and was known as the Puerto Rico Emergency Relief Administration (Administratión de Ayuda de Emergencia de Puerto Rico) known popularly as "La Prera". The second agency was founded in 1935 and was named the Puerto Rico Reconstruction Administration (Administratión de Reconstucción de Puerto Rico) known by everyone as La Prá". 14/ Under the supervision of these two agencies funds were provided for schools, roads, dorms, reforestation projects, public libraries as well as rural electrification. One of the more beneficial results of these New Deal Programs was that hundreds of young professionals participated for the first time in programs of social usefulness and acquired a great deal of experience."15/

World War II, however, was the catalyst toward prosperity for Puerto Rico. Money poured into the island to build or enlarge military bases such as the Roosevelt

Roads Naval Base, Fort Buchanan, Ramey Air Force Base, The San Juan Naval Station, Fort Allen and Sabana Seca. The construction of the military bases helped the island economy, but just as important was the money used to improve the infrastructure which was needed to provide necessary services to the military bases. A highway was built around the island to link the bases, electric power plants were constructed and water systems were improved or built for the first time. An elaborate system of communications was established all over the island for the military, and some of these were available to the civilian population. The bases also provided employment for Puerto Rican workers.

Another factor was that the draft (Compulsory Military Service) was launched in 1940, and it applied to Puerto Ricans as well as mainlanders, because they were American Citizens. Tens of thousand of Islanders were recruited for military service and served with distinction in the Pacific, North Africa and Europe. Some of these servicemen returned with pro-American sentiments but others returned with attitudes hostile towards the United States.16/

Regardless of their perceptions "vis-a-vis" the United States, the military services provided employment for thousands of young people and whether they spent their money on the island, or whether they sent money home to their families from the United States, or from some other overseas locations, the local economy received a tremendous shot in the arm. This process has continued up to the present, even though the North American Military has been greatly reduced with the closure of some military bases. Military service also contributed to social change on the island, because Puerto Rican veterans received the benefits of the G. I. Bill. This helped the veterans who served during World War II, but also in subsequent wars fought by the United States. This money also provided funds for local colleges and universities to expand and improve their facilities. This process of providing education to veterans also provided a boost to the industrialization process, because the colleges and universities offered programs needed by the new industries.17/

In the 1940's under the leadership of Luis Muñoz Marin, the leader of the Popular Democratic Party, the island began to industrialize. In 1946, President Truman named Jesus T. Piñero as the first Puerto Rican governor of the island. In 1947, the congress approved an amendment to the Jones Act which allowed the Puerto Rican people to elect their own governor. In 1948, Luis Muñoz Marin was elected.

In 1950, the congress of the United States authorized the election of a constitutional convention in Puerto Rico. The members were elected in 1951, the majority were members of the Popular Democratic Party and a minority of Statehood Republican and Socialists were elected. The Independence Party refused to participate.

The Convention met from September of 1951 to February of 1952. A referendum was held on March 3, 1952, and the proposed constitution was approved by a margin of 374,649 votes to 82,923. Under the new system of government, the governor of Puerto Rico received powers similar to those of state governors on the mainland. The biggest change, however, was that prior to 1952, the United States Congress had the power to approve, reject or change legislation approved by the Puerto Rican legislature. Under the new system the congress did not have this power.

The "Estado Libre Associado", or free associated state in English, was the name given to the new system of government which went into effect on July 25, 1952. The formula ratified the concepts of self government and of a permanent union with the United States.18/

In 1967, a status plebiscite was held on the island which allowed Puerto Ricans to express their opinion in regard to the future relationship between Puerto Rico and the United States. The purpose of this plebiscite, in the minds of the leaders of the Commonwealth party, was some sort of separate sovereignty in free association with the United States, in other words, a culmination of the process that they had been working towards.

In order to carry out this process a commission on status was elected and was composed of both Puerto Ricans and mainlanders. The commission on status then celebrated hearings, on the island to determine what the Puerto Rican people envisioned for their future. The results of the election gave 60% of the vote to the Commonwealth status, 39% for statehood and less that 1% for Independence. The last statistic is misleading, however because the pro-independence supporters boycotted the election.19/

The results of the plebiscite were seen as a victory for everyone according to their own point of reference. The Commonwealth Party viewed the results as a mandate for the culmination of the commonwealth status, the Statehooders viewed the results as their first victory against the Popular Democratic Party and the Puerto Rican Independence Party (which had not participated in the plebiscite) viewed the results as a victory, because of the massive abstentation of their status sympathizers, as a matter of fact the most important result was that the Statehood Republican Party split over the plebiscite issue.

The President of the party, Miguel Angel García Méndez rejected the plebiscite and refused to participate, another group of the party under Luis A. Ferré decided to participate and as a result of their success formed the new Progressive Party which won the elections in 1968, Luis A. Ferré, being elected governor.

Many Americans are aware that their school districts receive large injections of Federal Funds, but not many realize that programs such as Head Start; programs for students with learning and physical disabilities; language learning programs; chapter I; and scores of others are also funded in Puerto Rico. At the college and university level there are also a multitude of programs funded by the Federal Government.

In years past, college and universities received Federal Funds for specific items such as laboratory equipment, library books, dormitories, classroom buildings, etc. Later, the congress of the United States adopted a new policy in which students would receive a voucher, or grant, directly from the government which could be used at the college of the student's choice. The most well known and most utilized of these grants is the Pell Grant (named after former Senator Claiborne Pell, of Rhode Island). The grant is also known as the Basic Educational Opportunity Grant, and known in Puerto Rico as the BEOG.

The Stafford Loan program is a federal loan, it is a low interest loan made to students attending college at least on a half time basis. Another loan program is the Perkins Loan Program which is available to both undergraduate and graduate students.

In addition to the Pell Grant and the various loan programs there is also the Supplemental Educational Opportunity Grant which is awarded to students with exceptional financial need and it doesn't have to be repaid.

Another type of financial aid is the college work study program (CWS). This program provides jobs at or near the institution the student is attending. The pay will be at least the current Federal Minimum Wage, and it may be related to the type of work the student does and the skills required to do a particular job.

Other programs which are applicable to Puerto Rico are the programs for Veterans such as the Montgomery G. I. Bill which affected everyone enlisting after July 1, 1985. In each of the military services there are similar programs, but there are some differences.

The basic problem with these programs is that they are (or were) administered on a sort of "honor" system and are often poorly supervised, if at all. In New York, for example, some schools were receiving money illegally for students who were ineligible for grants or for students who didn't exist. These abuses have also been present in Puerto Rico. A few years ago, World University, with several campuses on the island, was found to have been using Federal Monies received from Puerto Rican students to fund programs for a branch of their university in the Dominican Republic.

Another example, is that of a student, whom we shall call "Magna Cum" a student at a university in the eastern part of the island, who registered every semester for 13 or 15 credits, after his tuition was paid by the Federal Grant, he would receive a refund for the difference between the actual tuition and the amount authorized by the Pell Grant. In addition he received money from the College Work Study Program (CWS). The problem was that he didn't attend classes and every semester he withdrew from all of his classes without a penalty or failing grade. His grade report simply listed W's in place of grades.

A more serious form of financial abuse of the grants is that of affluent families whose children receive the money even though they are ineligible. Because the grants are based on family income, students are obligated to show proof of family income by producing yearly income tax forms. Students and their families have found many ways of cheating this system. Parents might send a son or daughter to live with grandparents who are receiving social security, unemployment or disability payments. The student becomes eligible for a Pell Grant or some other form of financial assistance based on the income of the grandparents rather than the parents.

According to Alex W. Maldonado, a highly respected journalist in Puerto Rico, "ninety percent of the tuition paid by students in the private universities of Puerto Rico comes from Pell Grants".20/ In another local newspaper, **El Nuevo Dia**, Leonor Muller revealed that "Puerto Rico with a population of 3,700,00 has more post-secondary institutions (of learning) than any state of the union, and is third after New York and California in Pell Grants, but twenty-sixth in population".21/

Some institutions have employed educational representatives who are paid a commission and receive from one hundred to two hundred dollars per student admitted to a post-secondary institution. There are also schools where almost 100% of the students are admitted without having a high school diploma.22/

One of the really peculiar things about higher education in Puerto Rico is that the upper and middle class students attend the public university, which has lower tuition, while the poorer students attend the private, more expensive institutions. The reason for this is that the upper and middle classes can afford to send their children to private schools where they receive a much better education, whereas students from the lower economic levels must attend the public schools which for the most part do not prepare students very well for college. Students from the private schools perform much better on the College Board exams and are accepted by the University of Puerto Rico. On the other hand, students from the public schools are accepted by the private universities eager to obtain federal funds. The students are usually in open enrollment programs.

An interesting part of federally funded post-secondary programs is that the federal government expects the universities to pay for their laboratory equipment, building, computers, etc. from the tuition paid by the students. The result has been that post-secondary institutions are constantly raising their tuition costs and the federal government increases the amount of money for the various programs, resulting in a vicious circle.

The public university in Puerto Rico has not followed the same pattern because of politics. The government is afraid to raise the tuition because the upper and middle class students are led by their pro-independence leaders who threaten to strike whenever a tuition increase is mentioned. Some professors who favor independence (and who receive most of their salaries from the federally funded tuition) also support the strike threats for political reasons.

Alex Maldonado, in an article entitled the "Saga of a tuition increase" cited a study by Dr. Ramón Cao, Head of Economic Research for the Social Science Adjustment at the University of Puerto Rico. Dr. Cao discovered that the tuition at the University of Puerto Rico was about one-third the cost of public universities in the continental United States.23/

According to the story, the Council of Higher Education in Puerto Rico voted a tuition increase for the university of Puerto Rico for the academic year 1992-93. A typical undergraduate student with 15 credits would pay $690.00 for tuition, after the increase and $688.00 in fees, books, laboratories and a medical plan, for a grand total of $1,378.00. This seems reasonable for a full semester, one would think, comparing this with costs of mainland public universities, but in fact, the student would pay nothing, for he or she would receive a Pell Grant from the U. S. Treasury in the amount of $2,070.00. Simple arithmetic shows that the Pell Grant is $752.00 more than the cost of the tuition and fees - this is the famous "Reembolso" (refund). Not only does the student not pay, but he or she receives a refund.24/

On March 6, 1993, Robert Friedman examined the programs in an article entitled "Puerto Rican students eligible for Service Programs."25/ According to Friedman some $286 million dollars were awarded to students in Puerto Rico. This information was based on statistics from the United States Department of Education. This amount was expected to increase to over $300 million in 1992. 26/ In June of 1992, the Ponce Campus of the Inter American University revealed in its annual report that 96% of the students received economic assistance from the Federal Government. According to the figures, $7,537,337 was awarded in Pell Grants to 3,889 students. Students at the Ponce Campus were also awarded funds from other Federal programs; $193,026.00 was awarded to 633 students from the Supplementary Economic Grant (SEOG); $130,650.00 was awarded to students 27/ from the Perkins Grant; in addition, the College Work Study program (CWS) was awarded to 1,126 students and $1,896,985 dollars were loaned to students under the Stafford Loan Program.

If the United States government grants these huge sums out of generosity or a feeling of obligation to the people of Puerto Rico, who after all are American citizens, all well and good. It should be remembered, however, that a much higher percentage of students on the mainland are not eligible, because of the income of their parents. The truth is that students whose parents have to pay tuition are penalized, because the universities keep raising their tuition in anticipation of increased federal funding for needy students and this anticipation raises the tuition for the others. If these federal programs were not available the tuition would be a lot lower. Clearly there is a need for closer and more stringent supervision of these federal programs.

In the status debate, one of the most incredible arguments is that of international sports. In 1948, Puerto Rico became an independent sports entity, and has since competed under its own name and its own flag. Puerto Rico competes in such international events as the Central American games, the Pan American games, the Olympic games and recently, Puerto Rico broke with the United States in tennis and now has its own Davis cup team.

The argument is that under whatever status, Puerto Rico will continue to have its own sports teams - even if it becomes a state. Douglas Zehr, reported in a San Juan Star article that the results of a survey of Puerto Rican men revealed that 73% of the respondents argued that under no circumstances would they accept Puerto Rico losing its own Olympic representation. 28/

According to A. W. Maldonado, the argument as to whether Puerto Rico as a state could or could not keep its own Olympic Committee and participate in international sports, is more than a sports or legal issue - it is "a serious cultural issue". Maldonado's point of view is based on U. S. Census figures which predict that in 17 years Hispanics will be the second largest minority group and that by the middle of the twenty-first century nearly one of every four United States residents will be Hispanic.

What does all this mean to Puerto Rico and its relationship with the United States? Maldonado's theory is that "...as Hispanics become politically dominant in certain areas (Florida, Southern California and the Southwest) the shrinking American (Anglo) majority will want to ensure that this does not lead to having a distinct cultural nation within the United States. If in the future the government of

Puerto Rico should go to Washington with a mandate for statehood, Puerto Rico will be asking to be entered into the Union as a Hispanic state- 'We want our own Olympic team because we are different; oh yes, we are loyal American citizens and we want to be a state, because we want all the rights and obligations of 100% citizenship.' But we want to retain our international sports identity and we are determine to keep it and protect it. 'What is more important in this Olympic matter is not whether what the State holders are promising is realistic or not. It clearly isn't. The message is in the asking and as the implications of the United States census figures on the rapidly growing Hispanic population sinks in, it doesn't take much imagination to foresee what the reaction will be throughout the United States. The message being sent is; we want to be a state, but we do not wish to be Americans.'" 29/

In another article by María Bird Picó entitled "All Parties Stroke the National Identity - Nationalism" she wrote that "while three political parties are selling a different status for the island, there is a common thread in that their message is 'Puertorriqueñidad'." In the same article Ms Bird Picó stated that "the Popular Democratic Party used the recent "Las Americas" basketball tournament to unveil the first, plebiscite TV spot, which says that Puerto Rico as a state would not be able to participate in the Olympics. Governor Rosselló meanwhile has tried to reassure islanders that Puerto Rico would seek to participate in international events as a state. 31/

In another article in the Star, Javier Maymi quoted the governor as saying "that if Puerto Rico should become a state, its Olympic identity will not be bothered. 'We don't need permission from the United States to do anything. I think that the relationship to Olympic sports is a great one. This is a situation much like the Catholic Church. The church in Puerto Rico answers to the Vatican not to the government. The Puerto Rico Olympic Committee answers to the IOC (International Olympic Committee) not to the government'." 32/   In past rulings, however, the International Olympic Committee has taken identity away from countries that became part of another nation. A precedent was the annexation of Latvia, Estonia, and Lithuania by the U. S. S. R. These countries lost their representation and their athletes had to compete for the Soviet Union. In the Caribbean, Martinique and Guadalupe, which are integral parts of France, do not participate in regional or Olympic contests. The question is: whether the United States will admit Puerto Rico under special conditions? The answer seems to be no. A former senator from New Jersey, Bill Bradley, a famous ex basketball player for Princeton University and for the New York knicks, has said that if Puerto Rico becomes a state and gets its own Olympic Committee, "I will lobby for New Jersey to get its own Olympic Committee."33/ As a matter of fact, the Puerto Rican sports identity has a legal obstacle. "The Amateur Sports Act of 1978 states that only the U. S. Olympic Committee will have a say on Olympic matters in the country."34/

Benny Frankie Cerezo, a former statehood representative, in an article entitled "Plebiscite Campaign Flawed Cultures" stated that the admittance of Puerto Rico as a state is the acceptance of Puerto Rico as an equal and the acceptance of the proposition that the nation will become pluralistic, multinational, and different. "I think it will be a better nation, but congress should think whether it will."35/

The simple fact is that the emphasis on international sports participation is based on nationalism. At the Olympics in Barcelona, Puerto Rico won a single bronze medal in boxing, but Gigi Fernández, a well known Puerto Rican tennis player competed for the United States and won a gold medal. She was crucified locally for her failure to represent Puerto Rico.

The best way to describe some of the sports officials who favor Olympic participation is simply to call them charlatans who want to travel to such luxury locations as Barcelona, Rome, Tokyo, London, etc., at the expense of the poor Puerto Rican taxpayer. Usually there are more officials that there are athletes at international sports events. Much of the money that could be used to help the athletes ends up in the entertainment fund for those who accompany the athletes.

Puerto Rico continues to produce outstanding athletes, such as Chi Chi Rodríguez in golf, Gigi Fernández in tennis, and Roberto Clemente and Orlando Cepeda in baseball. In a new generation we have the Alomars, "Igor" González, Carlos Baerga and Edgar Martínez to mention only a few. The majority of the most successful island athletes have honed their skills in the United States where there is a greater opportunity to receive specialized coaching; in addition the athletes have access to better equipment and better competition.

The key to the sports argument is nationalistic and culturalism. Nationalism as was seen in the ex-Soviet Union and the ex-Yugoslavia was a divisive factor, and the truth is that the United States needs more unifying factors or we will become the ex-United States. Until the Korean War, Puerto Ricans fought in their own military unit, the much decorated 65th Infantry Division. Since then they have been assigned to completely integrated units where American Nationalism is emphasized.

Jorge Luis Medina, the San Juan Star's "Video Psycho" recently criticized the relationship between sports and culture by saying that Puerto Rican culture should not be "five bozos playing basketball".

15

One of the most emotional issues in the relationship between Puerto Rico and the United States is that of Language. In 1991, when the Puerto Rican government, under then Governor Rafael Hernández Colón, approved a "Spanish - only" law, there was a strong reaction both in favor and against. The purpose of the law was to establish Spanish as the one official language of Puerto Rico, prior to the passage of this law, both Spanish and English had been the official languages. English was reinstated as one of the official languages when the pro-statehood party gained power. The Spanish only law caused reverberations not only in Puerto Rico, but also on the mainland. Patrick Buchanan's reaction was that "it should warn the United States that the taking into the union of a people with a distinct cultural identity is asking for serious trouble"36/ Buchanan further predicted that such a "bad marriage" will lead to a "bloody divorce."37/ He also pointed to an ominous sign in California, where a United States English group was assaulted by some Hispanics who were shouting "Spanish should be the spoken language".38/ Maldonado himself, referred to Spanish - only as a slap in the face, and asked "How can one seem to be against the English language without being seen as anti - American".39/ He referred to the language issue in another article entitled "Lost in America", in which he stated that "nothing so stirs (American) animosity toward Hispanics as the belief that they don't wish to learn English"40/

A typical gut reaction was that of Donald S. Hoseur, at the American Legion National Convention held in Phoenix, Arizona in 1991. Hoseur, upon learning of the Spanish - only bill, "Introduced a resolution upon the United States to give independence to Puerto Rico, because with Spanish - only, Puerto Rico couldn't function within the United States."41/

A majority of Panelists at the National Press Club discussing bilingualism and public policy believed that the English - only movement in the United States had a hidden motive of restricting the immigration of Hispanics and Asians. On the other hand, the Spanish - only law in Puerto Rico was described as a means to uphold the Hispanic tradition. James Crawford, one of the panelists who opposed the English Language movement as xenophobic, admitted however, that "the Puerto Rican law was adopted in a special political context at the time of the status debates and the motive was not to uphold some sacred mission, but to kill statehood."42/

If politics was the motivating force for the Spanish - only law, then it succeeded. Ex - Senator J. Bennett Johnston of Louisiana, who headed the committee responsible for implementing a status plebiscite in Puerto Rico, described the Spanish - only bill as a "particularly clumsy thing to do." He continued, "I fear that the other members will...sort of say, they want to be different and therefore they're not our responsibility, thinking of themselves less as Americans and more as some Hispanic Caribbean Country."43/ The plebiscite was finally scuttled by the senate committee which voted 10 in favor and 10 against holding the status plebiscite. Melinda Karl tells the story about an English language advocate group which planned to run advertisements in island newspapers calling for Puerto Rico to remain "separate" from the United States after enacting Spanish as its first official language. The group also claimed to be sending letters to its members stating that it might be time to cut U.S. ties with Puerto Rico altogether and give the island its independence. The letter read "that it might be time to listen to the voices in

Puerto Rico that 'hate America' and insist on their own separate language and culture..."44/ The letter also read that "helping Puerto Rico become an independent nation would solve a number of problems, including illegal aliens using Puerto Rico as a stepping stone to the mainland and the terrorist threat posed by some pro-independence groups on the island."45/

A favorable reaction to the Spanish - only law was that of Ricardo Alegría, an anthropologist, who said that "language is more than just speaking; its the way you think. We make love in Spanish, we talk to God in Spanish...it's vital for the culture."46/ He also went on to say that "I personally was famous at the university of Puerto Rico for the many times I flunked English."47/ In Puerto Rico, questioning the "supremacy of Spanish can be akin to burning the flag. The mother tongue is the symbol of cultural identity."48/ It appears that Alegría may be indebted to the Emperor Charles V of the Holy Roman Empire who supposedly used different languages for different purposes, but spoke to God in Spanish.

An interesting aspect of the Alegría case is that the American government recently gave him an award for his contributions to American culture - a culture he has fought against all his life. Even Rubén Berrios, the Puerto Rican independence leader, was astonished at his acceptance of the award and he was even more astonished when Alegría decided to vote for the Commonwealth option in the referendum, supposedly to help the independence option.

Another point of view is that of Glynn C. Moran, who pointed out that the founder of the English only movement was none other that S. I. Hayakawa, a Japanese - American and former Senator from California.49/ Moran's idea is that the United States is unique in that its citizens are representatives of every race, nationality, religion, creed, culture, and language on earth. The two characteristics which bind us into a cohesive hole are our constitutional democracy and our use of English as our common language. The commonality of our use of English is a catalyst which makes us American. According to Moran, the primary opponents of the English only movement come in two plummages:

1)Professional guilt laden liberals who are convinced that anything that might help America is criminal.

2)Some minority leaders who fear the loss of their own jobs should their immigrant constituents become proficient in the language of the land and no longer need the patronage of the local "jefe"50/

Rafael Hernández Colón, the Governor of Puerto when the Spanish - only bill was signed, "never once said that the bill eliminated English as one of the two official languages of Puerto Rico since 1902."51/ The governor always formed his explanations "in terms that could lead listeners or readers to think that Spanish was finally made Puerto Rico's official language after 91 years of struggle."52/

To put the language argument into its proper perspective it is helpful to look at the argument of a former Puerto Rican legislator, Bennie Frankie Cerezo. His point of view is that Puerto Rico cannot enter the union as a separate entity with its own Olympic team, its own language, etc., and this should be thought out by Congress. "The admittance of Puerto Rico as a state is the acceptance of the proposition that the nation will officially become pluralistic, multilingual, and different. It will not be the same. The powerful Hispanic caucus that will emerge, the powerful network of Hispanics arising out of Puerto Rico's acceptance as an equal will change the United States forever."53/

The language issue in Puerto Rico is a mirage. The truth is that in Puerto Rico, there is an English speaking elite that learned English at good private schools in Puerto

Rico and then graduated from stateside universities such as Yale and Harvard. They then send their children to the same schools. Naturally, they speak only Spanish in the home or with friends, but they owe their jobs and status to the fact that they know English. The language is also extremely effective in keeping out North Americans, because in order to get a job here, one must speak Spanish. The hypocritical part is that the elite send their children to private schools, but they don't want their children to have to compete with the lower classes, so they sabotaged the teaching of English in the public schools.

The lower classes have never understood this, because the elite have blinded them with nationalistic arguments and their defense of the mother tongue. The lower classes believe in the malarkey preached by the leaders of the Commonwealth and Independence parties.

The language policy of the Popular Democratic Party has been an educational disaster. The reason is that the universities use a majority of English language texts, especially in the sciences, Business Administration, and advanced courses, which the students do not read, and if they wanted to, couldn't. Even worse, many of the professors teaching the courses in which these textbooks are used do not understand them either, and the result is that the students are tested only on the notes taken in class, which are in Spanish. If the texts were in Spanish, this disaster might be averted, but they are not, therefore many university graduates have failed to master their disciplines.

Recently, the Young status bill has created a controversy of major proportions on the Island. The author of the status legislation is Representative Don Young (R-Alaska) who favors statehood for the island.54/ He has been able to achieve a bipartisan interest in the "decolonization" of Puerto Rico in the House Resources committee of which he is the chairman.55/

The two most controversial issues of the bill are United States citizenship and the language issue. The language situation may become an issue if "House Rules Committee chairman Gerald Solomon (R. New York) attempts to amend legislation to read that only under statehood can English be the island's one and only official language and the language of instruction in public schools. Even if Solomon's effort gets nowhere, the Young bill implies a transition to English for the island over the years. It says that any transition toward statehood should 'promote the usage of English by the United States citizens of Puerto Rico...' it also notes, that, as in other states, statehood for Puerto Rico should mean that English would be 'the common language of understanding.'"56/ The Clinton Administration's position is opposed to this type of legislative language, because it would create 'divisiveness" and "that Puerto Ricans should not be denied statehood, and the full rights of citizenship ... because their principal language is Spanish, instead of English.57/

Since the victory of governor Pedro Rosselló in the election of 1996, his secretary of education, Victor Fajardo, has begun the implementation of a plan, whereby mainland, teachers will be brought to the island as exchange teachers for Puerto Ricans who will in turn teach in the United States. The objective is to improve English language instruction on the island. This plan has stirred up a violent reaction, according to the results of an island poll, "more that 90 percent insisted on using Spanish exclusively in private and official dealings with the Puerto Rican and U. S. Governments. The survey also revealed that more than 75 percent of Puerto Ricans, have a negative attitude toward the English language..."58/

Elsa Tío writing in El Nuevo Dia claimed that by using English as the language of instruction Puerto Ricans would be "asfixiarnos espiritualmente" (suffocated spiritually).59/

She went on to say that English instruction would be a blow again to the people's self esteem. A more violent reaction was that of Renán Soto Soto, the President of the Federation of teachers, who announced that "Vamos a soltar las avispas" which roughly translated means that the American teachers would stir up a wasps nest.60/

A somewhat more reasonable reaction was that of the sportsman "Fufi" Santori who argued that it is much easier for elementary children to learn the language that they have been learning at home. He also pointed out that, "al inglés se le conoce como 'el dificil' y lo es" in other words that English is more difficult to learn because it is not phonetic.61/

The fact remains that language remains as one of the most volatile elements in the question over U. S. Puerto Rican relations and may be the deciding factor in determining what those relations will be in the future.

During the fiscal year 1990, the island received a total of $1,169,110,841.00 from the Federal Nutritional Aid Program, 62/ which is known in Puerto Rico by its Spanish Acronym PAN.63/ This aid included $936.8 million in the "PAN" program and $232,310,841 in the Women, Infants and Children's Program (which is known as "WIC"), the National School Luncheon Program and Programs for the elderly, etc. 64/ In the Fiscal year 1995, Puerto Rico received $1,478,000,000.00 from the "PAN" program and 85 million in nutritional assistance for children, according to the U. S. Department of Agriculture.65/ The Republican welfare reform plan for fiscal year 1996 called for a 15% increase in food assistance to Puerto Rico, to $1,698,000,000.00 and a 100% increase in nutritional assistance for children, to $170 million dollars.

The Federal Nutritional Aid Program was extended to Puerto Rico in 1974. In 1981, about 1.8 million people or 56% of the island's population received money from the program at a cost of $915 million. The "PAN" program has a cap, which in the case of Puerto Rico, is about 64% of full funding, 66/ but Guam, the Virgin Islands and the Northern Marianas get full food stamp allowances. The Northern Marianas also receives, full SSI (Supplemental Security Income) funds, but Puerto Rico, the Virgin Islands, Guam and American Samoa do not 67/ Robert Friedman of the Star Washington Bureau estimates that if the cap were lifted, Puerto Rico would receive another $700 million in the "PAN" program and if the SSI were applied the island would receive another $900 million.68/

In the United States, 35 million Americans live at the subsistence level with one of ten in the nation receiving food stamps, while one out of six New Yorkers receives food stamps.69/ In Puerto Rico, six out of ten people receive food stamps, meanwhile the United States was accumulating debts to the tune of $400 Billion a year 70/

In the status plebiscite of November, 1993, all three of the political options in Puerto Rico - Statehood, Commonwealth and Independence - endorsed the idea of an increase in Federal Funds and the elimination of the Cap on the "PAN" program. Partisans of statehood say that Puerto Rico would receive an additional 3.7 billion over the present 8 billion for various programs. In addition, if President Clinton's Health Program had been approved, the island would have received an additional $300 million to help small businessmen pay for the health care of their employees. Independence advocates argue that the United States should continue to pour Federal Funds into the Republic of Puerto Rico as an indemnity for 95 years of occupation.71/

The supporters of Commonwealth want to restore recent cuts in the 936 program and to include the island in the Supplementary Security Income for the aged, the poor and disabled. They also request the elimination of the cap on the "PAN" Program.72/ Former governor, Carlos Romero Barceló (now the Resident Commissioner in Washington, D.C.) was able to convince the congress to change the "PAN" Program. Formerly the recipients received food stamps, but now they receive a check which has probably contributed to the abuse of the program. It is much easier to use the money to buy rum, or drugs or even gamble, instead of using the money for food. It is entirely possible that the United States taxpayer is contributing to the rising crime rate in Puerto Rico.

A. W. Maldonado wrote an interesting article entitled "Lost in America," for the San Juan Star, 73/ the article features the book of Ms Linda Chavez, entitled Out of the

<u>Barrio - Toward a New Politics of Hispanic Assimilation</u>. Ms Chavez writes about the different Hispanic groups living in the United States which includes a devastating chapter about the Puerto Ricans living on the mainland. According to Ms Chavez, there is a case to be learned in the case of the Puerto Rico because "More that any other group they are hooked on welfare."74/ Another important statistic is that "41% of New York Puerto Ricans have parents that were also on welfare."75/ She also points out that "back on the island, 70% of all islanders get some form of assistance."76/

On November 8, 1993, "Time Magazine" published an article entitled "Puerto Rico: State of Anticipation" referring to the plebiscite of November, 1993. The article reviewed the various status options and quoted Governor Pedro Roselló who promised that for every new tax dollar going to Washington, three would return in the form of higher assistance under statehood.77/

Senator Rubén Berrios, of the Independence Party joked that "It is not a matter of give me statehood or give me death. It is a matter of give me statehood so I can have more food coupons."78/

SECTION 936/006

Probably no aspect of United States - Puerto Rican relations has had more publicity and is less understood than the famous or infamous Section 936 of the Internal Revenue Code.

The ancestry of Section 936 (Section 931) was established in 1921, by the congress of the United States to promote investment by United States Companies in the Philippine Islands. Section 931 was later applied to other U. S. Territories and Federal taxes were exempted until the dividends were repatriated to the United States. In 1976, the congress changed the exemption to a credit. The idea was to promote employment in Puerto Rico, so for every person employed, the company receives a credit which reduces their obligations to zero. Ex-Senator David Pryor, from Arkansas, a leader of those opposed to Section 936, argued in Senate debates that the "island's pharmaceutical companies receive an average of $70,788 in Federal Tax Credits for each employee, while the employee only earns an average of $26,471,"79/ "The highest ratio per employee was Pfizer with tax savings of $156,400 saved for every employee earning an annual average of $25,000, while Schering registered the lowest savings of $48,417 per employee."80/ The United State treasury claims "to lose about $3 billion in taxes annually from Puerto Rico's 936 companies, 55% of this amount is attributable to the pharmaceutical."81/ Pryor said that a new federal study "clearly and undeniably illustrates that the American government has given the pharmaceutical industry a blank check to pillage the federal treasury through Section 936."82/

An interesting feature of Section 936 is that if

companies repatriate their earnings immediately, they incur a reduced credit, but if they deposit their earnings in island banks they do not. Dennis Rivera, the most powerful Puerto Rican labor leader on the mainland, serving as President of the New York based local 1199 of the Drug, Hospital and Health Care Employee's Union stated that: "The United States is going through its most difficult process, one that parallels the 1930's. The nation faces a new millennium in which one out of three jobs is under the poverty level."83/ Rivera added that Section 936 generated $12 billion for local banks. "There's no place in the United States that has $12 billion generated by 936 companies to play and finance."84/

Federal Funds received by Puerto Rico have been increasing rapidly during the 1980's and 1990's according to A. W. Maldonado. During the past decade, Puerto Rico has received $56 billion from the United States, not counting the tax dollars lost to the federal treasury because of section 936.85/ While billions of dollars are poured into the bottomless pit of Puerto Rico, industries in the United States have been steadily vanishing. One can question "the unfairness of a federal taxation system that allows companies with gigantic profits to repatriate them without paying taxes, while the product being manufactured becomes more and more expensive in the United States market."86/

Doreen Hemlock wrote an interesting article in the San Juan Star, which referred to a book entitled America: What Went Wrong? by Harold F. Barlett and James B. Steele, which appeared on the "New York Times" bestseller list (Barlett & Steele are reporters for the "Philadelphia Inquirer"). The book investigated how practices in Washington and on Wall Street have benefitted only a few Americans (according to Lewis Lopham in his book: (The Wish for Kings: Democracy at Bay, 90% of the wealth of this country is in the hands of 5% of the population). Barlett and Steele made the claim that Section 936 of the United States Internal Revenue Code "amounts to a U. S. Taxpayer subsidy for companies to export jobs to lower - wage Puerto Rico,"87/ with 936, they estimate, "The United States, loses up to $60,000 a year for every $6.00 an hour created in the pharmaceutical industry in Puerto Rico. Thus it would be cheaper for the United States government and all American taxpayers to send annual subsistence checks to those island residents who work for American drug companies and keep the jobs here (in the United States)."88/

An example quoted by Ms Hemlock, from Barlett and Steele, is that of a worker, George Shelton, who lost his job to a runaway plant and has difficulty understanding the Washington wisdom underlying the tax breaks: "Everybody says 'Well, they're (Puerto Rico) just like a state': Well they're not just like a state cause they don't pay taxes and our state sure in Hell don't get those kinds of tax breaks."89/

In another article entitled "Commonwealth at 40", Robert Friedman pointed out that $90 billion or so in federal funds have flowed into the island since 1970, and according to the U. S. Census Bureau and Planning Board figures Puerto Rico received a yearly high of $8 billion last year.90/ Still other observers argue that while U. S. taxpayers shell out the federal aid dollars to the island. U. S. businesses shoved them back into their own coffers. Between 1982 and 1989, the 936 companies made more than $40 billion in profits, according to figures obtained from the Commonwealth Treasury Department.91/ Other "studies by the United States Treasury Department and Congressional Budget office indicate that the Federal Government would get between $2.5 billion and 3.5 billion a year if the 936 companies paid U. S. Corporate income tax. Since companies in the United States pay up to 34% in corporate income taxes - this means that 936 companies are probably earning between $7.5 billion to 10.5 billion in yearly profits. 92/

As David Pryor said about the situation, "It is outrageous that our revenue code contains a legal loophole - the section 936 tax credit with billions of dollars to the pharmaceutical industry. It is unconscionable that working Americans and businesses must continue to subsidize the most profitable industry in the nation when there are so many other unmet social priorities."93/

Recently the Section 936 argument has been partly resolved. On August 20, 1996, congress cut off the income-based credit for new businesses and began to phase out the program so that the industries currently benefitting from Section 936 would gradually lose their tax breaks to the tune of $4.9 billion in eight years.94/

The idea of congress to repeal Section 936 was to help reduce the budget deficit and to replace the income-based income with a wage-based credit. Money that the federal government would receive from the pharmaceutical and other companies would be used to help pay for the new Small Business Protection Act of 1996. This act is designed to provide businesses with new tax breaks and is using the repeal of Section 936 of the Internal Revenue Code as the primary revenue raising offset for these tax breaks"95/, according to Carlos Romero Barceló the Resident Commissioner. The Political manipulation on the part of the Statehooders here is clear. As long as Puerto Rico benefitted from Section 936 people would vote against statehood knowing that residents of Puerto Rico would have to pay taxes as well as losing their 936 benefits. The Commonwealth Party favored Section 936 for the opposite reasons.

The Resident Commissioner's argument is clear - "If

Puerto Rico were treated as a State, in Medicaid alone we would get more than $1 billion per year."96/ This of course doesn't mention other federal, funds which Puerto Rico has not been deemed eligible, or programs which are capped at a certain level such as the Food Stamp Program. If these were factored in Puerto Rico would receive "an increase of $1.34 billion in federal benefits...would boost our GNP by almost 2%."97/ There are those who would argue that once the residents of Puerto Rico pay into the Federal Treasury the imbalance will disappear. The fact is that very few residents will pay taxes and the imbalance will remain approximately the same.

A rather depressing part of modern life is listening to our nation's leaders, the media and talk show hosts. Their use of cliches and childish jargon is particularly disheartening. One of the more recent favorites is the so-called "level playing field." For those of us who are fortunate enough not to listen to our nation's leaders or talk show hosts, the level playing field means that no participant in the game of life has an unfair advantage over the other participants.

If this definition is used then there is no level playing field in U. S. Puerto Rican relations. Ex-Senator Victoria "Melo" Muñoz, the 1992 candidate for governor of Puerto Rico, for the Commonwealth Party told reporters that Puerto Rico was not always trustworthy in its relationship with the United States Congress.98/

One of the examples used by Senator Muñoz was the perceived failure of Puerto Rico to set up effective regulations that would bar U. S. Companies from bringing runaway plants to Puerto Rico in order to receive tax benefits under Section 936. A runaway plant, according to our definition, is a factory that decided to relocate in Puerto Rico, and closes an equivalent factory in the United States, leaving its former employees without jobs. A legitimate move, is one in which a company adds a new factory in Puerto Rico, but the old one remains open.

Robert Friedman asserted that a total of 23,664 workers in the continental United States lost jobs at 59 factories because of so-called runaway plants that have relocated in Puerto Rico. 99/ The study on which the article was based was released by the Midwest Center for Labor Research, a non-profit labor group. The study conducted on behalf of the Oil, Chemical, and Atomic Workers International Union. The union was in the forefront of lobbying for legislation to stop businesses from relocating to the island to take advantage of the 936 program. The study shows "an overwhelming pattern of tax-loophole-driven job destruction," according to MCLR Director Greg LeRoy. "This study ends the debate about whether many 936 shops are runaways. 'They are,' said LeRoy."100/

The investigation, "which includes 50 case studies, concludes that runaway plants have caused the loss of 56,342 indirect jobs for a total statewide loss of 80,000 jobs."101/ According to the study, "the companies taking advantage of Section 936 are typically large Fortune 500 firms which transfer their 'intangible' assets to the island for tax write offs."102/

Jorge Medina, in another article, quotes Dennis Rivera, the Puerto Rican labor leader as saying "...U. S. Industries have been steadily vanishing... Where once there was a thriving steel industry that employed over 1.5 million, less than 100,000 steel workers remain. Television sets are no longer manufactured in the states. The company that manufactured Schwinn bicycles moved abroad; the pharmaceutical industry practically moved to Puerto Rico."103/ It is in that context that one ought to look at Section 936.

An important case, which illustrates the runaway plant situation, was that of Whitehall Laboratories in Elkhart, Indiana (the owner of American Home Products). According to the Oil, Chemical and Atomic Workers Union, 104/ the company transferred most of its production facilities to its Guayama Plant in Puerto Rico with plans of shutting down the Elkhart facility and putting about 800 employees out of work. The allegation was also made that federal funds were used in the construction of the factory in Guayama and for the training of its workers. The union and its allies also focused on the Puerto Rican law that grants 936 benefits to qualifying plants. The law had a provision mandating that the governor deny such benefits when a plant transfer to Puerto Rico would cost jobs on the mainland, however, the government of Puerto Rico has never denied tax benefits to any plant. Representative Pat Roberts (R-Kansas) attacked Section 936 and Puerto Rico in a letter to a colleague. Roberts used as his most important example the case of Hays, Kansas, a small town which sought to convince a pharmaceutical and medical instrumentation manufacturer to locate there, instead it went to Puerto Rico! "The city's efforts have been unsuccessful because tax incentives, available for locating in Puerto Rico outweigh the fundamental costs of production."105/

In other words, the tax writing efforts of congress have helped Puerto Rico while causing unnecessary dislocation in Kansas and other states.... Put more simply, the federal government through tax policy has diverted industry from a struggling state to alternative locations."106/

According to the union the following jobs were lost on the mainland:

1.American Home Products, October 1990, closed their Elkhart Plant - 800 workers were laid off.

2.Cheeseborough Ponds announced the closing of a perfume plant saying it would move to Puerto Rico.

3.West Lynn, Massachusetts - some 2000-3000 workers lost jobs at a General Electric Turbine plant in the 1970's. It moved to Puerto Rico.

4.New Brunswick, New Jersey - more than 1,300 workers lost jobs at an E. R. Squibb Pharmaceutical plant due to its transfer to Puerto Rico.

5.In October of 1988, Smith, Kline and Beacham and Beacham closed one of its drug plants in Philadelphia: 800 workers lost their jobs to Puerto Rico.

6.Letitz, Pennsylvania lost 180 jobs when Warner Lambert transferred to Puerto Rico.

7.Johnson & Johnson laid off 350 people between 1988 and 1990, in Bridgewater, New Jersey in a move to Puerto Rico.

8.When Carter Wallace Medical Products moved to Rincón, Puerto Rico, Cranberry, New Jersey lost 200 union jobs.

9.DuPont laid off workers in Garden City, New York when they transferred their operations to Puerto Rico in 1987.

10.When Westinghouse closed their circuit breaker plant in Bridgeport, Connecticut, 450 employees lost jobs to Puerto Rico.

11.Bristol Myers laid off 200 production workers from their Syracuse, New York plant when they moved to Puerto Rico.

12.DuPont closed its electronics plant in Niagara Falls, New York, in February 1990 to move to Manati, Puerto Rico.

13.DuPont closed a chemical plant in Jonesboro, Arkansas in October 1987, and transferred their operations to Puerto Rico.

14.Two hundred workers in Irvine, California lost their jobs when Allergon moved to Hormigueros, Puerto Rico.107/

The lawsuit against American Home Products was finally settled out of court for $24 million, but the company did not admit guilt.108/

A. W. Maldonado, the great apologist for Section 936 believes that plants that move from the mainland to Puerto Rico are acting legitimately, because in the United States a plant may close in Connecticut and move to North Carolina. The fact that he overlooked is that North Carolina cannot offer the incredible advantages that Section

936 offers mainland companies which transfer to Puerto Rico.

Naturally the Section 936 companies have had a powerful lobby in Washington, the Puerto Rico - USA Foundation (PRUSA), to protect their profits. Carl Nordberg, the executive director of PRUSA attached an article that appeared in the Wall Street Journal that was critical of Section 936. According to the Journal, Section 936 would have been eliminated earlier if it had not been for the lobbying of PRUSA.

In addition to federal funds for such things as education and nutritional assistance Puerto Rico and the other territories have been recipients of a broad array of some 300 federal assistance programs"109/ some of which may be unknown to the public and probably to many members of the congress, from 1970 to 1991, "some 90 billion or so in federal funds have poured into the island 'according to U.S. Census Bureau and Planning Board figures'."110/ In 1991, Puerto Rico was receiving approximately 8 billion a year, but that figure has now reached "10 billion annually"111/

Another advantage to the U.S. Connection is "Puerto Rico's ability to sell bonds and notes on Wall Street in order to raise funds for the development of the island's infrastructure and is absolutely the key to its growth. Puerto Rico is the 'Shining Star of the Caribbean' precisely because it can tap into the stateside and international markets in ways that other islands and countries cannot. Consider that the island's public debt now stands at 12.54 billion (revised estimate today stands at approximately $14 billion) and nearly all of that is in bonds now in that the hands of institutional or corporate investors who enjoy, federal, state and local tax exemptions."112/

Puerto Rico also receives aid for damages caused by natural disasters. The island received $576 million or 74% in grants and a total of $881 million in federal relief"113/ with the help of the Federal Emergency Management Agency (FEMA) in the aftermath of Hurricane Hugo in September of 1989.114/ South Carolina received $1 billion in total aid, the Virgin Islands received $610 million and North Carolina $69 million, but most of the money was in loans, only $202 million in the three areas was in grants. A South Carolina "fire chief" David Phillips lost his home and wanted FEMA to help. 'All I wanted was $1,500 to put in a new septic tank'"115/ (not approved)

In Puerto Rico, on that the other hand, Gabriel Alvarez Gonzáles, a 46 year old truck driver lived in a wood and tin shack. He received $25,000 package of federal grants. Alvarez built a three bedroom concrete house containing new appliances, matching living and dining room sets and a couch with a built in tape deck and stereo speakers. A stereo speaker by itself was considered a luxury which FEMA wouldn't allow, "but we looked around and were able to find one built right into that the couch."116/ Alvarez explained: "I could never in my entire lifetime have done anything like this."117/

One South Carolinian remarked that "either people in South Carolina were grossly under-compensated or that the people in Puerto Rico were grossly over-compensated."118/ It also should be mentioned that the damages sustained by South Carolina were greater than in Puerto Rico, an interesting aspect of that the story is that Puerto Rico has tough hurricane building laws. Most of the houses there are built of concrete so Hugo destroyed mostly the old wooden structures.

Another advantage, which helped fuel the industrial growth on the island is the fact that Puerto Ricans do not pay excise taxes. For example, Puerto Rican rum is taxed in the United States to the tune of about $200 million a year, but that money is returned to that the Commonwealth government annually.119/

Recently, before the health reform program was defeated by the Republicans and the health insurance companies, Governor Pedro Rosselló received confirmation from first lady Hillary Clinton that Puerto Rico would be included in the administration's national Health Care

Plan.120/ Puerto Rico would (according to the plan) have received approximately $300 million to be used as subsidies to help, small businesses to pay the medical plans of their employees. Carlos Romero Barcelo said "that Puerto Rico could expect as much as $1.2 billion a year if it were included in that the program."121/

In the plan proposed by the president there was a proposal to cover part of the cost of the program by raising the tax on cigarettes by 75 cents a pack, but Puerto Rico would not have been obliged to pay because it would be an excise tax.122/

The aforementioned programs do not include other benefits such as public housing funds, money for highway construction, salaries paid to federal employees on the island, or funds for the National Guard or the Armed Forces Reserve. It also does not include money spent by the army or navy to build facilities on their bases by local contractors, etc. Roosevelt Roads Naval Base received almost a direct shot from Hurricane Hugo and the destruction was enormous. A great deal of money was spent on repairs to the base which also helped the local economy.

Every year Puerto Rico has been receiving an increase in Federal funds. The island received $6,143,000,000 in 1987, and in the fiscal year 1993-94 received an estimated $9,040,469,000 which represented an increase over that the fiscal year 1992-93 of 5.1%123/

This situation is not unique to Puerto Rico but is related to the crazy concept of zero based budgeting where there is an almost automatic increase in costs of all federal programs every year and is one of the main reasons for the enormous federal deficit.

A significant factor in the status debate in Puerto Rico is that of nationalism, over the years there has been a rapid development of educational institutions that have educated the doctors, lawyers, teachers, business executives, bankers and the leaders necessary for the successful functioning of an independent nation state. This is the same process which occurred in the British North American colonies between the 1740's and the 1770's. According to Carl and Jessica Bridenbaugh, in their book <u>Rebels and Gentlemen: Philadelphia in the Age of Franklin</u> the colonies were dependent on Great Britain in the 1740's but by the 1770's the colonists had matured to the point that they could function on their own.124/

The same process has taken place in Puerto Rico. Ricardo Alegría, a former head of the Institute of culture laments the fact that the North Americans tried to force him to learn English from North America teachers who were imported to teach in the island's schools. The truth is that under the Spanish, there were no universities on the island and only a couple of secondary schools. The result was that there were practically no Puerto Rican teachers prepared to teach (in whatever language) in the educational system launched by the North Americans. It was for this reason that teachers were imported from the mainland. This process was also repeated in the Catholic parochial schools.

As universities were established on the island and teacher training programs were instituted, North American teachers were gradually replaced by local teaching personnel. Today there are practically no North American teachers at the public school level. At the same time, private schools were established to provide English language instruction to the children of North American executives working on the island. Gradually the North Americans were replaced by islanders who began to send their children to the private schools not only to get a better education than was provided by the public schools, but also to learn English. The result is that today, Puerto Rican children make up the vast majority of students in the private schools. This process takes place even in the military base schools which accept not only the children of Puerto Rican military personnel, but also civilians with no connection to the military.

There are fewer American business executives than before. When new businesses are established, American executives are sent to the island to get their business going and to hire and train local workers. This is true not only because of the language situation, but also because it is cheaper to hire locally. If Warner Lambert transfers an executive to Puerto Rico on contract, the company has to provide transportation, not only for the family, but also for the furniture, car and cat. Once on the island the company may find it necessary not only to pay a higher salary than on the mainland, but also to pay for the education of the children. In the past, the locals lacked the technical skills necessary to work in the new pharmaceutical and electronics industries, but with the federal assistance for university students providing the money necessary to establish university programs, it is now possible for the companies to recruit locally.

The truth is that the vast majority of the federal government employees working on the island are Puerto Ricans, including many of the top administrators. The reason is that in practice, the federal employees need to be bilingual and few mainlanders qualify, but even if they did, they probably would not be hired. An interesting item is that the federal employees receive a COLA (Cost of Living Allowance), supposedly, because the cost of, living is higher than on the mainland. When it was suggested that maybe the COLA should be eliminated, Jaime Fuster, the ex-resident Commissioner, argued that the federal employees had to send their children to private schools to study in English, even though the vast majority of the federal employees are islanders who could do very well in the public schools. Needless to say, the COLA is still in effect.

The growth of nationalism has been an evolutionary process which has taken place not only on the island, but also in the large Puerto Rican community in the United States. In the elections of 1992, and 1994, three Puerto Ricans were elected. Nydia Velázquez and José Serrano of New York and Luis Gutiérrez of Chicago. The latter favors independence for the island, when he visited the island after his victory, he received a hero's welcome from the local "independentistas". He also made it clear that his constituency stretches beyond the 500,000 Puerto Ricans living in Chicago. "I have a strong commitment to them, but I also want to learn how I can help to improve the quality of life and to do justice for all Puerto Ricans."125/ His ultimate constituency, he said, "embraces the five million Puerto Ricans in the 'Diaspora' all over the continent."126/ Gutiérrez also stated that "all political prisoners in federal captivity...be released".127/ The political prisoners evidently included the "macheteros" responsible for the $7.1 million Wells Fargo heist in Hartford, Connecticut. The "macheteros" were the ones who claimed responsibility for the slaying of two United States sailors near the Sabana Seca Naval Base in 1979.128/ Gutiérrez was also involved in getting approval and money for a statue of Dr. Pedro Albizu Campos the leader of the Nationalist Party in Puerto Rico, which led an attack against President Harry Truman and later wounded some representatives in the House of Representatives building in Washington D.C. - a cartoon appeared in the Chicago Sun Times referring to the incident. In the cartoon the statue arrives at a park in Chicago and a workman tells the delivery people to put the statue "over there next to Oswald and Booth."

María Bird Picó tells the story of "Seva", which illustrates the negative attitude of many Puerto Ricans towards the United States. Ms. Bird quotes a short story written by Luis López Nieves. The story is about a historian who discovers that United States forces landed in May 1898, in a town called Seva, instead of in July 1898, in Guánica. Supposedly, news of that event was squelched, because the troops were greeted by fierce fighting by Puerto Rican troops (the opposite of what happened). In anger the United States troops later exterminated the town, building a military base over it and renaming it Ceiba (Roosevelt Roads Naval Base is located in Ceiba). The piece was first published in Claridad (a pro- independence newspaper) in 1983, without any indication that it was fiction. It caused a wave of reaction that "was so overwhelming that the story quickly became a matter of study among island intellectuals. 'Seva is us - a true nation over which a false one has been superimposed' said poet José Miquel Torres... a few attributed the outpouring to the willingness of Puerto Ricans to believe the worst about the United States. There is a collective mentality of screwing the United States..."129/

In a related article also by María Bird Picó nationalism was also emphasized. "The most surprising is that the-statehood movement would play the nationalistic game, 'They all sound like independentistas,' quipped one observer, and the the-statehood governor, Pedro Rosselló, appointed an "independentista" to head the Puerto Rico

Institute of Culture, which receives a significant amount of federal dollars, which it uses to glorify Spanish culture."130/

A. W. Maldonado commented on the position of George Will, who believes that bringing Puerto Rico into the union with a distinct cultural identity is asking for serious trouble. George Will and Patrick Buchanan have been buttressing their points of view with examples such as Northern Ireland, French Canada, Yugoslavia, India and the ex Soviet Union. Nationalistic conflicts between - different ethnic and religious groups in some of these countries have caused and in some cases, continue to cause atrocities and civil war. The big problem with Puerto Rican statehood is language, "Americans should say diverse things, but should say them in a common language which allows universal participation in the conversation."131/

Another ingredient in the status argument is the island's intelligentsia. In the plebiscite of November 1993, the independence option received only 75,000 votes but many party faithful either didn't vote, or voted for the commonwealth party in order to deny statehood a majority, a large number of intellectuals on the island classify themselves as "independentistas". The significance is that the vast majority of the population may favor either the commonwealth or statehood options, but the fact remains that the spirit of nationalism is present in all three status options and this will always present a problem for the United States.

At the heart of the nationalism issue is the question of citizenship. In the status debates Rubén Berríos the spokesman for the independence option proposed that Puerto Ricans be granted dual citizenship if Puerto Rico should be granted their independence.

The origin of the citizenship argument goes back to the Foraker Act of 1900, which ended the military government of the United States and recognized Puerto Rican citizenship. This status was verified by the case of González v. the United States. Isabel Gonzalez was refused entrance to New York on August 24, 1902, because she was a foreign immigrant. The U.S. Supreme Court ruled that Puerto Ricans "had the condition of nationals that was distinct from that of American citizens and that permitted their access to the United States as citizens of Puerto Rico."132/ The key to the debate is whether or not the Jones Act of 1917 abolished Puerto Rican citizenship, when U.S. citizenship was granted to the islanders. Mari Bras the Dean of Puerto Rican Independence leaders argued that it was not abolished and therefore remains in effect.133/

The citizenship argument became an issue in 1993, when "Fufi" Santori "signed a sworn statement rejecting his U.S. citizenship. His example was followed by about 300 other independentistas among them Mari Bras,"134/ The statements were not accepted because all "legitimate renunciations had to be done in a U.S. Embassy, in a foreign Country."135/ To make a long story short, Mari Bras traveled to Venezuela in the U.S. Embassy in Caracas, and returned without incident to Puerto Rico.136/

Juan Mari Bras followed up his renunciation of U.S. Citizenship with his avowed intention of voting in the November, 1996 election. San Juan Superior Court Judge Angel Hermida ruled that it's a violation of the commonwealth Constitution to make American citizenship a requirement to vote in Puerto Rico."137/ The core of the nationality argument was stated clearly by Judge Hermida when he wrote: "that those born in Puerto Rico ... constitute a community with an identity, culture and sovereignty and that the members of that community define themselves precisely as Puerto Rican."138/ In an informal Star poll conducted on the ruling by Judge Hermida, a majority of the respondents favored the ruling. An example was the opinion of Sixta Piña Centeno who said: "It was an accurate decision. In my opinion the main citizenship is the one we have here [of Puerto Rico]."139/

The citizenship debate will continue to be one of the factors that the status commissions will have to take into consideration in planning for future plebiscites on the island and whether or not the spirit of nationalism can be reconciled, or will lead to independent nationhood.

In the United States congress there some who are opposed to statehood for Puerto Rico, as well as those who are in favor, the main factor in determining who they are is political in nature.

If a national referendum were held in the United States, in which American citizens were allowed to vote in favor, or against statehood, there would probably be a large majority in favor.

Those in favor of statehood for Puerto Rico, both on the island, and in the Congress of the United States use some of the follow reasons for their support: First, with approximately 3.7 million people, Puerto Rico ranks among the first ten countries of the world in their purchase of American products. Puerto Ricans buy more than a billion dollars of goods from the United States annually.

Second, the geographical location of Puerto Rico has been and continues to be important for both strategic and commercial reasons. While the location of Puerto Rico is not indispensable for the United States, particularly after the collapse of the Soviet Union, it is, nevertheless, very important in maintaining and protecting the shipping lanes both to the United States and to the Panama Canal. In the - the year 2000, the treaties for our bases in Panama and Cuba will expire and conceivably this may leave Puerto Rico as the only United States base in the Caribbean.

Third, Puerto Rico, because of its Hispanic Origins serves as a territorial ambassador between Latin America and the United States. The use of Spanish and English, as well as its geographic location have been important factors in the development of our relations with Central and South America.

Fourth, since 1917, when Puerto Ricans became American Citizens, they have participated in all of the wars in which the United States has found itself. Puerto Ricans have served with distinction in both world wars, as well as in the conflicts in Korea, Vietnam, Grenada, Panama and the Persian Gulf.

A fifth reason is the fact that as time has passed there has become a more integrated relationship between the island and the mainland. To begin with, Puerto Ricans belong to professional, social and fraternal organizations in the United States. The island's economic, financial and banking systems have become intertwined with those institutions on the mainland. Programs such as Social Security and Medicare are applicable in both countries and are programs that Puerto Ricans do not want to lose under any status option. The educational system of Puerto Rico is another example. To begin with, the island has used the American model in the development of their universities and many Puerto Ricans study in mainland institutions. Puerto Rican – institutions of higher learning are accredited by mainland accrediting agencies. This relationship between Puerto Rico and the mainland has become even closer as a result of computerization and more recently the connection between educational facilities and the Internet.

The integration of the two entities is also seen by the following examples: Puerto Ricans travel freely to and within the United States and the United States Postal Service serves the island as well as the mainland. In addition, Puerto Rico is subject to the controls of federal agencies such as the F.C.C., the E.P.A. and the F.B.I. Puerto Rico's maritime, land and airspace are subject to the control of federal agencies as well as immigration and security. An important factor is the integration of the American military machine with that of Puerto Rico, not to mention the military bases. These factors, now in place, would make the acceptance of Puerto Rico as a state much easier. It would also make it more difficult for Puerto Rico to become an independent republic because a separation would cause a major disruption.

Another development, which needs to be considered in the acceptance of Puerto Rico as a state or as an independent republic is the fact that even though Puerto Rico would become the poorest state in the union, the economic situation has improved to the point that the income per capita has become the highest in all of Latin America, therefore, the transmission towards statehood, independence, or some sort of associated republic would pose no serious problem to either the United States or Puerto Rico, as long as the process is gradual.

Arguments against statehood are also important to take into consideration. One of the most important is – the political factor. The first of these political considerations is the fact that Puerto Rico would be represented in the United States Congress by two senators and seven representatives, most likely democrats. The addition of seven representatives may result in the reduction in their number in other states. "In a poll of ten southern governors, six were in favor of Puerto Rico as a state, but others opposed the idea for various reasons, Governor Cecil Underwood of West Virginia said that his 'only concern is how much representation West Virginia could lose' noting that his state has lost three representatives over the past four years.' Governor Kirk Fordice was even more outspoken, when asked the question, he replied, 'Let's be real selfish: I'm a Republican, and it (a 51st state) would diminish Republican Strength in the United States, number one. Number two, it (a Puerto Rican state) would bring more non-English speaking people into the United States and I think that is a big problem."140/ Trent Lott, the majority leader of the Senate said recently that he "opposes island statehood, because Mississippians could lose their own voice in congress if Puerto Rico becomes a state. He said that the state would surely lose a House seat if Puerto Rico is admitted as a state."141/ Carlos Romero Barceló said that "the fear among the Republican leadership in the senate that Puerto Rico could become a Democratic state 'has been a determining factor' in blocking passage of status legislation."142/ The other argument against statehood is that the addition of nine Hispanic legislators would create a more powerful lobby in the congress, an idea which would be opposed by some as a movement away from assimilation and toward a multi-cultural nation. The political factor delayed the admission of Arizona and New Mexico and later, Hawaii and Alaska.

The economic factor is also important because Puerto Rico would be the poorest state in the union and federal assistance program money would increase and this would more than offset the amount received by the Internal Revenue Service in income taxes. This is true, because some federal programs are capped at a certain level or are not applicable to Puerto Rico under the present system of government.

Another reason that may prevent Puerto Rico from being granted statehood is the fact that their traditions, customs and past are different from those of the united States. The United States has traditionally absorbed those immigrants who have entered the country. They have adopted the English language and in several generations or less have lost their former languages, Language then is a major obstacle for statehood, because the Puerto Ricans want to preserve their language. If the congress of the United States should decide to impose English as the official Language as a condition for admission as a state this might cause the Puerto Ricans to reject the statehood option.

One of the reasons that may affect the situation is that some Americans and some members of congress are unhappy about is the tide of legal and illegal aliens, the majority of whom are from Latin American countries. In recent years this tide has become a flood, not only in the United States, but in all of the industrial nations. This has caused a reaction in our country which can be referred to as nativism. In 1992, the candidate who best represented this attitude was Pat Buchanan.

It is highly unlikely that congress will act on project H.R. 3024, introduced by congressman Don Young of Alaska, which was introduced in February of 1996, to hold another status referendum in Puerto Rico. This status Referendum will not be adopted as long as the republicans have a majority – in the senate, they assume rightly, that the democratic party would dominate the island's elections. Some Republicans opposed the admission of Alaska on the basis that they would elect democrats, but they favored Hawaii, because they assumed that the islands would vote Republican and vice versa. The fact is that Hawaii has tended to vote democratic and Alaska has been voting for the Republican party candidates.

The present Governor, Pedro Rosselló has decided that Puerto Rico should hold their own status plebiscite on December 13, 1998, at which time the Puerto Rican people will be able to vote for all four status options. The idea is that the United States can accept or reject the status chosen by the people of Puerto Rico, but if they should reject that decision, it would be obvious to everyone that Puerto Rico is a colony of the United States. When push comes to shove the United States has made it known that Puerto Rico is a non-incorporated territory, which is in fact a colony. The fiction promulgated by the United States in November of 1953, that Puerto Rico was no longer a colony meant that the United States no longer needed to provide a written report to the United Nations on the status of Puerto Rico. If the United States rejects Puerto Rico, this fiction will be revealed.

Many pro-statehood Puerto Ricans, including the Resident Commissioner Carlos Romero Barceló have expressed their intention to opt for independence if statehood is refused by the states.

In a recent book, <u>La Gran Decepción</u>, Dr. Enríque Vásquez Quíntana includes a chapter entitled "Accidentes en la Politica de Puerto Rico"./143 The first of these so-called accidents occurred before the Spanish American War. This was the famous "La Carta Autonomica", or charter of autonomy, which was granted by Spain to Puerto Rico on November 25, 1897. The Charter was related to the struggle of Cuba for her independence. Spain feared that Cuba would obtain her sovereignty as a result of a military conflict with the United States. For this reason the Spanish prime Minister Praxedes Mateo Sagasta, granted a charter to Cuba and later to Puerto Rico. The Cubans realized that the charter did not provide sovereignty for their island and opposed it, the Puerto Ricans on the other hand, felt satisfied with what they considered to be an improvement in their political situation.

The Charter was never ratified by the Spanish legislative body, because the prime minister wanted it to go into effect before the outbreak of war with the United States. The truth is that the Charter gave absolute power to the governor of Puerto Rico, who was nominated by the king of Spain. The governor had the power to veto laws approved by the legislature of Puerto Rico and the laws that were approved had to be submitted to the Spanish legislative body for ratification. The administration of justice and commercial treaties remained under the control of the Spanish Government, in other words the Spanish maintained complete sovereignty over the island. Under the Charter, Luis Muñoz Rivera became the Prime Minister of Puerto Rico. The new assembly met on July 17, 1898 and was dissolved after the American invasion on July 25,

1898.

The second accident was the annexation of Puerto Rico by the United States, which according to Vásquez Quíntana, was taken by accident, in order to pay for the costs incurred by the United States in the Spanish American War. The reality is different. In the first place there was a group of Puerto Rican professionals living in the United States who were described by Angel Rivero in his book <u>Crónica de la Guerra Hispano Americano en Puerto Rico</u>, as a group of pro-American annexionists who were admirers of the United States. This group included Julio J. Henna, Roberto H. Todd, Matteo Lluveras, Mateo Fajardo and Dr. Rafael del Valle among others. They actively lobbied with Senator Henry Cabot Lodge of Massachusetts and Theodore Roosevelt to intervene in Puerto Rico and annex the island. They also provided important information concerning the Spanish military forces on the island and other information concerning their armaments, bridges, roads and railroads. The said that they not only wanted to cooperate with the United States forces but that they wanted to serve in those forces if and when they were to invade Puerto Rico./144

Senator Lodge heard them with interest and recommended that they talk with Theodore Roosevelt who was the Secretary of the Navy. When they met with the secretary, he indicated that although he was in charge of the preparations for a probable war, he had never thought about Puerto Rico./145 Later, Dr. Henna and Roberto H. Todd, president of the "Club Separatista Rivera de Nueva York" met again with Roosevelt and the War Committee. Roosevelt told them that if there should be a war, "el Ejercito de los Estados Unidos opéraria contra la isla."/146 The truth of the matter is that Puerto Rico had always figured prominently in Roosevelt's plans, because he was interested in acquiring a naval base on the main island or on the island of Culebra.

After the island was ceded to the United States, it can be seen that the United States had parted from tradition. For the first time the United States did not promise the rights, advantages and immunities of American citizens that it had made with Louisiana in 1803, with Florida in 1819, with New Mexico in 1848, with Hawaii in 1898 and with the Philippines in 1898. In all of these territories the United States promised to grant statehood or independence. For the first time, in Article IX of the Treaty of Paris, the United States did not commit itself in regard to the future of Puerto Rico./147

On May 1, 1900, the American government established what is known as the Foraker Act, which created a civil government in Puerto Rico. It was decided that the system of government would be similar to the one that was planned for the Philippines Islands. The Foraker Act did not create an independent state nor did it provide American Citizenship to the inhabitants of the island. In other words they were without rights. The Foraker Act did not contain a Bill of Rights and did not mention a single individual liberty. The law for the Philippines did contain a bill of rights and other advantages not contained in the Foraker Act. Don Luis Muñoz Rivera said that the Foraker Act violated all of the Principles of the American Constitution, because it failed to separate the executive power from the legislative power./148

In 1901, in the case of Downes v. Bidwell, the Supreme Court of the United States decided that the status of Puerto Rico was that of a non-incorporated territory (which is what it remains today). What can be said is that the Foraker Act did not create a definite status for Puerto Rico and did not create any options for the future. Dr. Vásquez Quíntana considers the Foraker Act to have been an accident, because it was the result of the imperialistic mood of the moment, which was of short duration.

Some persons consider the Jones Act, which granted American citizenship to the Puerto Ricans in 1917, to have been an accident, because of the fact that it coincided with the American entry into the World War. Some independence supporters believe that American citizenship was granted in order to make the Puerto Ricans serve in the military forces of the United States. This was not the case, because citizenship for the islanders had been under discussion since 1910.

In 1916, the Congress of the United States had given the Philippine Islands a new governmental system and promised to give the islands their independence as soon as they were able to establish a stable government. On the contrary, the Jones Act made no reference to eventual independence for Puerto Rico.

In 1952, the "Estado Libre Asociado de Puerto Rico" known in the United States as the commonwealth of Puerto Rico, was approved. The idea of the Associated Free State had been considered by the "Partido Union de Puerto Rico", in 1922. In 1942, Rafael Cordero, Enríque Campos del Toro and Miguel Guerra Mondragón, members of the Popular Democratic Party, discussed the concept of the Associated Free State with the North American governor Rexford Tugwell. He was of the opinion that the island was not prepared for statehood and that the Commonwealth government could serve as an intermediate status before statehood. The idea was that for these three leaders of the Popular Democratic Party, the Associated Free State was a step in the direction of statehood.

In 1967, the Popular Democratic Party and the Commonwealth status won a victory in the status plebiscite, although the advocates of statehood, claimed a moral victory, because their vote was larger that before. The Popular Democratic Party was unable to capitalize on their victory, because they lost the general election of 1968, to Luis A. Ferré and the New Progressive Party.

From 1989 to 1991, the Congress of the United States celebrated public hearings, which were intended to resolve the status problem of Puerto Rico. The House of Representatives approved the project, but the Senate didn't take action, therefore, nothing was resolved. In 1993, a new plebiscite was conducted without any commitment on the part of the United States Congress, the result was a victory for the Commonwealth status.

It seems that whenever a political status seems to have a possibility of success, the Congress of the United States has not been receptive to the idea. Another impression is that whenever a political party tries to resolve the problem of status, a new party is created, such as in 1967, or in 1984, with the party of Renovación. Another possibility is that the independent voters or the indecisive voters move in a contrary direction and change the electoral results.

The "Escape Valve" in this chapter, refers to the immigration of Puerto Ricans to the United States, as well as to other countries, such as Ecuador, Peru, Cuba and Santo Domingo after the Spanish American War.

The first phase of this outflow was between 1899 and 1902. Approximately 6000 Puerto Ricans, almost all from the coffee growing region of the island left under contract for Hawaii as agricultural laborers. These workers who were promised better conditions of work, found that the conditions were close to slave labor. The majority of them never returned to Puerto Rico. The United States government encouraged the immigration, because of the belief that Puerto Rico was over populated.

After the initial departure of workers for Hawaii, this immigration tapered off. The second phase, between 1902 and 1917, saw some contract workers leave for such locations as Ecuador, Peru, Cuba and Santo Domingo.

The third phase began in 1917, the year the United States entered World War I and the Jones Act extended American citizenship to the island. The shortage of labor in the shipyards and war industries was an incentive for the immigration, the federal government also got into the act by contracting many workers to work on the mainland. Thousands of Puerto Ricans worked in those industries between 1917 and 1918, and even though a recession occurred after the war, the immigration continued when economic prosperity returned in the early twenties. This immigration was encouraged by the fact that the United States had drastically reduced the number of foreigners permitted into the country. The combination of these factors stimulated the demand for immigrants and being citizens enabled the Puerto Ricans to enter without difficulty. A third factor was the high unemployment on the island that stimulated workers to immigrate.

The immigration of Puerto Ricans to the mainland in those years between 1930 and 1945, decreased to a trickle as a result of the depression and World War II. After the war, however, there was a shortage of labor in the industrial sector, particularly in the metropolitan area of New York. Many companies sent agents to Puerto Rico in order to recruit workers directly. Independent agencies on the island also sent workers to the mainland in order to relieve the shortage. "Richard Wagner the Mayor of New York visited Puerto Rico in 1953, and encouraged the immigration to New York by saying that' !Habiá trabajo para todos!"/149

The Puerto Rican government played an important role in the immigration by establishing some safeguards for those workers and regularizing the process. The government fulfilled the function of intermediary between the workers and mainland employment. In part, immigration was encouraged to provide an escape valve for the excess population of the island. At the same time birth control was encouraged by the government.

The Popular Democratic Party, which was in control of the government acted as an intermediary in three ways. The first method was to increase air travel between the island and the mainland, as well as to keep the ticket costs as low as possible. Second, was to disseminate notices all over the island concerning job opportunities available in the United States. Third, was to establish some standards for the treatment of Puerto Rican workers. This was particularly true of seasonal workers. In some places, such as New York, the Puerto Rican government established offices that helped immigrants and attended to their claims.

The statistics on immigration are impressive,

particularly after 1945. The estimated statistics are based on the number of passengers arriving or leaving the island in a given year, mostly by air. If you assume that the tourists will cancel themselves out with their round trip tickets you are left with either an increase or decrease in the number of immigrants or immigrants. According to the estimates only 1,800 left during the depression years and 4,600 between 1941 and 1945. These numbers increased after the war reaching a yearly average of 31,000 in 1946-50, and 45,000 in 1951-60. The largest number in a single year was 1953, When 75,000 Puerto Ricans left the island. In the years 1961-70, there was a decrease in the number of immigrants averaging 16,500 a year, this reduction was caused by a decrease in employment on the mainland and increased opportunities on the island./150

It is important to note that sometimes more people returned to the island than immigrated. This is known as the "migración de retorno"./151 Many studies have been conducted concerning this phenomenon and they indicate that those people returning to Puerto Rico come from all social classes and include professionals as well as day laborers. To me the reason is the magnetic attraction of the culture and the sunshine of the homeland. Another reason that many returnees give is to raise their children in a less hostile environment. Whatever the reason, they do return and in large numbers, but their numbers are almost eclipsed by the larger group who are leaving for the mainland. In a given year 50,000 "Newyorricans" may move back to Puerto Rico, but 90,000 islanders move to the United States./152 In addition to flights to and from New York, there are flights to Hartford, Chicago, Philadelphia, Orlando and Miami.

One of the concerns in Puerto Rico is what the locals refer to as the "identity crisis". This "identity crisis" is found principally among those who travel back and forth and take their children with them. Some children are constantly being yanked out of school in New York and put in a school in Ponce or Mayagüez, the main problem being the fact that in New York they learn English and Spanish in Puerto Rico. The obvious result is that the majority of them have problems in school, Bilingual programs have helped many Puerto Ricans in New York, but there is less emphasis on bilingual programs in on the island. The "identity crisis" manifests itself, according to Marco Rigau, an island senator, because when "Newyorricans live in New York, (they) watch Puerto Rican television stations, go to the 'mercado' for Puerto Rican products in East Harlem. Here they live in Levittown, watch cable TV and eat Kentucky Fried chicken"./153 The Newyorricans tend to favor statehood or the Commonwealth status rather than independence. To the average Puerto Rican the philosophy of independence remains emotionally appealing, but seems impractical. The independence movement has become largely a cause of the educated elite, which makes schools a key to the movement. On the Mainland independence sympathizers can be found among the small Puerto Rican population on Ivy League campuses. "Independentistas" like to call these schools "colonialist universities, but they attend them. Pedro Albizu Campos went to Harvard University. Rubén Berrios Martínez, the current nonviolent independence leader, has a Yale Degree"./154

Many years ago, when the author lived in Aguadilla, a nephew of a close friend was a student in an Ivy League college and later was offered a teaching position at Wesleyan University as well as at Princeton. Every year he would visit his parents in Puerto Rico, but he never stayed for more than four or five days, because he missed the cultural events in New York City. He was a member of the old Partido Socialista Puertorriqueño, a more radical independence party than the present one, the fact was that he was emotionally involved in the Puerto Rican independence movement, but he didn't want to live there.

Dr. Enríque Vásquez Quíntana, in his book, <u>La Gran Decepción</u>, points out that whatever political party wins an election in Puerto Rico, and becomes the governing party, will find the task much more difficult than a political party governing a state of the union. The difficulty is caused by the fact that Puerto Rico has not resolved the status question. This has caused political parties on the island to spend a great deal of time and energy in trying to define the future of Puerto Rico. The party which has found it the easiest to govern, is the Popular Democratic Party, because the "Estado Libre Asociado" is a creature of their creation. It is much more difficult for the statehood party, because they not only did they not create the system, but they reject it and want to become a state. The foundations of the "Estado Libre Asociado" were built during the governorship of Don Luis Muñoz and include health and education services, the electric company, the water company and until recently "Nuestra Telefonica" which was sold recently to an American company.

The former Popular Democratic Party governor, Rafael Hernández Colón discussed the problem of governance in an interview on July 26, 1993, with the well known journalist and political analyst Alex E. Maldonado of the San Juan Star. The gist of the interview was that the Puerto Rican government doesn't work. For someone who had been governor of the island for twelve years, this was a startling admission./155

The reason for this failure to govern efficiently can be seen by the fact that the governmental agencies, for the most part are slow, inefficient and treat the public with disdain. The agencies are like this because they have become so politicized and this has created an animosity among the personnel - of those agencies. This is all the more tragic because the government is the largest employer in Puerto Rico and because the budgets are limited, the salaries are low in comparison to the private sector. Rafael Hernández Colón related an incident in which he had visited one of the public corporations known in Spanish as the "Corporación de Vivienda Publica" which was responsible for public housing. The governor had visited the agency to try to resolve some continuing problems and the personnel accepted his ideas for improvement, but nothing happened. It wasn't until the services were privatized that those problems were solved./156 John Kennedy complained when he was president that his orders were often lost in the bureaucracy. He would give an order to the Secretary of State, for example, who would send memos to his subordinates for a change in policy, but when it was received at a lower echelon, the change was disregarded and the old policy was continued.

At one time the author was working with the various military educational programs in Puerto Rico and when orders were received to institute a new program or to emphasize the importance of education for advancement, the air force and the army would implement the changes immediately. The Navy, however, would respond affirmatively, but would do nothing. The reason for this is that the navy has never valued educational programs as much as the other military services. Some years ago, I visited the motor vehicle department in Mayagüez, Puerto Rico to purchase a car. All of the necessary papers were completed and in good order, but I was told to come back the next day. I returned only to find that they had lost the paperwork for the transaction and that I would have to go through the entire procedure again. Having anticipated that there might be problems, I had made a copy of all of the papers, the clerk told me, however that they couldn't accept copies and that I must supply only originals. In total, it took me eleven visits, before the deal was finally consumated. An interesting fact was that the office didn't even have any file cabinets and all of the records were stored in unalphabetized paper boxes on the floor. A few years later we hired a retired major who had worked as an administrator of a military hospital in Colorado. He asked me about registering his car and I explained where he should go, but I cautioned him that he might have some problems. After going to the office, I had sent him to, he was told that he could not register the vehicle there, but that he would have to go to another distant town. After two visits he was told that he would have to return to the original location, in all it took four visits for his transaction to be completed.

The list of problems with governmental agencies is endless, but a good example of the problem can be seen in the mandatory car inspection. Puerto Ricans must have their vehicles inspected on a yearly basis in mechanic's shops that are licensed by the government. Too my knowledge I never remember anyone actually having their car inspected. You simply go to the shop, the mechanic puts on a sticker and you pay the basic fee.

Dr. Pedro Rosselló the present governor, not only agrees with Hernández Colón about the governmental situation, but has decided to dismantle or privatize the huge public corporations. This can be seen with his sale of the telephone company to a private company. Rosselló's campaign is also aimed at lowering or eliminating the enormous debts which the governmental agencies have accumulated. "La Autoridad de Acreductos y Alcantarillados" (water and sewers) has a debt of over 8 million dollars. At the same time, the consumer has to pay his bills on time or be cut off. The governmental agencies are receiving money from the central government to keep operating./157

Governor Rosselló is following the example of Margaret Thatcher, who began to dismantle the socialistic enterprises in Great Britain that had been established by the Labor Party. The big advantage was that the government sold those enterprises for more than the debts, therefore they made a profit. The majority of the companies that were privatized began to make money after their sale. This same model was followed in Argentina and many other countries. The sale of "Nuestra Telefonica", a governmental corporation will eliminate the debt and produce a small profit for the government. It has also created a problem, because some of the employees of the other large corporations fear the change, especially those that are incompetent or do not like to work, therefore, their reaction has been negative.

The problem of having employees of different political parties working in different agencies and corporations has caused animosity and instability and a failure to provide proper services to Puerto Rican citizens. In the United States, if employees of different political parties work together it is usually in a harmonious fashion, except for an occasional flare up at election time.

The big problem is the fact that the Popular Democratic Party, which has governed for so long, was unable to amend or bring about a decision by the United States government to recognize the Commonwealth of Puerto Rico as the present and future government of Puerto Rico. The reason for this failure is the fact that the United States Congress "claims" that one congress cannot tie the hands of a future congress, and therefore, if the congress of 1999 or 2000 were to determine that the "Estado Libre Asociado" were to be recognized as the legitimate government of Puerto Rico for now and always, a future congress could nullify the agreement. This of course is hogwash, while it is true that they have the power, the fact is that we would be dealing with a moral commitment which we couldn't very well change.

PLEBISCITE/014

On December 13, 1998, a plebiscite was conducted in Puerto Rico with five status alternatives. The first alternative was the Commonwealth status or the "Estado Libre Asociado", the present form of government, which was defined on the ballot as a territorial commonwealth, in other words a colony. The Popular Democratic Party, for this and other reasons decided to opt for "none of the above", as a result this option received only 0.1% of the vote. Free Association, sometimes referred to as the Associated Republic involves a treaty between two sovereign nations. This option garnered only 0.3% of the vote. Independence, a third option, received 2.5% of the vote. Statehood received 46.5% of the vote, up from 46.2% in the previous plebiscite. The largest number of voters supported "none of the above" which received 50.2% of the votes and implied a rejection of the other four options. "It was the second time in six years that Puerto Ricans voted down statehood in plebiscites called by Rosselló and his New Progressive Party."/158

As usual in status plebiscites held on the island all sides declared victory. "The people have spoken democratically and have sent a clear message. The first thing the people said is that Commonwealth has ended, Governor Rosselló told supporters around 7 p.m., when the electoral results made it clear that the fifth column would win the election. "Today. . . statehood won. Statehood won."/159

The Popular Democratic Party also claimed victory, "over at the PDP headquarters thousands of Commonwealth supporters claimed a victory for Commonwealth."/160 Acevedo Vilá the President of the Popular Democratic Party, said that the "none of the above' column is not a petition for a status change, but a rejection of statehood."/161

The Puerto Rican Independence leader Rubén Berríos claimed that "Puerto Rican voters killed Commonwealth, the Current political status. . . Commonwealth was unanimously rejected by Puerto Ricans. Now we must look for the only real solution to the status issue, full sovereignty."/162

Free Association supporters also were optimistic about the results of the plebiscite. Pro ELA President Luis Vega Ramos "said that option would be the true winner in the long run, because the results were a clear sign of rejection of the current colonial status."/163 Even though the free association column received only 0.3 percent of the vote, Vega Ramos "said that the U.S. Congress will not grant statehood to the island nor will it continue to accept commonwealth. Therefore, a new definition must be presented and that could very well be free association."/164

The reactions from the United States reflected the confused message which was sent by the results of the plebiscite. A Clinton administration official issued a statement that noted that "while a vast majority of the votes among the status options were for statehood a majority of the total vote was not for any of the options."/165

One of the most interesting and intelligent reactions was that of Rep. José Serrano, D-N.Y., a Mayagüez born Bronx lawmaker. His reaction was that "I don't know how the people I deal with on a daily basis are going to figure this one."/166 Serrano agreed that the majority of plebiscite voters rejected statehood and any of the other sanctioned options, but added that "Popular Democratic leaders did not come up with an alternative, which is a major problem."/167 Serrano's opinion was that if the PDP leaders had backed the Commonwealth option on the ballot and had drawn a majority, they could have come to congress 'to negotiate something better. . . But it's going to be very difficult for 'none of the above' to get anyone's attention in Congress". He concluded his comments by saying: "If I sound confused it's because I am."/168

The meaning of the status plebiscite results were explained by Frank Ramos of the San Juan Star. He said: Last Sunday, in their infinite wisdom, the Puerto Rican people chose to postpone any decision regarding their political destiny. Given the confusion and the ambiguity surrounding all of the status alternatives currently on the table, it was a smart choice. In other words the voters' apparent indecision was the right decision. By marking their ballots for 'none of the above' a majority of the voters were saying, in effects, that they were not prepared to make a choice on their future political status, and that's mainly because their leaders haven't given them the information they need to make an intelligent decision"/169

Ramos recommends that at least five years should elapse before the next plebiscite, because the people need a respite "from the political status wars."/170 He pointed out that before the next plebiscite congress and not the local government should enact and define the process and the status alternatives and that the status legislation should include a commitment by congress to act on the results. He also recommends the revival of a joint U.S. Puerto Rico status commission that would include representatives of the different status alternatives as well as members of congress and the executive branch of the federal government. The commission would be charged with determining the status options and their corresponding definitions, to be included on the ballot .

Finally, the plebiscite "should be preceeded by an educational campaign, preferably one not controlled by the political parties. . . The purpose would be to give voters a clear, truthful idea of what each status option represents, free of partisan political propaganda."/172

The voters could not select one of the first four options, because they did not have the information to make a rational decision. The information that they needed included such things as to whether the commonwealth status can become permanent or is it transitory and will disappear? If we were to become independent, would we lose our citizenship and our social security benefits? And, what is free association? If Puerto Rico were to become a state, how much would it cost and would English be imposed against the people's will? These are only a few of the myriad questions to which there were no answers.

Another way of addressing the victory of "none of the above" is the failed strategy of the governor. If the new Progressive governor had dealt with the problem in an even handed manner, it is possible that the statehood option might have carried the day. If we look at the options themselves we are provided with some interesting concepts. The first is that the Free Association option was a creature of some of the left leaning members of the Popular Democratic Party. If one looks at the possibility of having both Free Association and the commonwealth status on the same ballot, the hope seemed to be that the party would split and this would have enabled the statehood option to win. Furthermore, the Popular Democratic Party has always argued that they are not a colony, that they are not an unincorporated territory, but on the ballot they were described as a territorial commonwealth. These two factors forced the Popular Democratic Party leaders to vote against their own favored option and vote for "none of the above". The failure to win a majority for statehood was explained by Governor Rosselló "As a protest against him and his Administration, but not a defeat for statehood."/172 He should have added that it was also a defeat for his strategy.

CONCLUSION

December of 1998, will mark a century of rule by the United States over Puerto Rico and many Puerto Ricans would like to see a final resolution to the seemingly eternal status question.

In order to make sense out of the process, it may be helpful to deal with certain facts or realities which may lead us to a particular solution.

The first fact that we have some evidence to support is that many Republicans do not want Puerto Rico to be admitted as a state, because of the fact that if Puerto Rico were to become a state of the union, the 2 Puerto Rican senators and the 7 Puerto Rican representatives to congress would in all likliehood be Democrats. This would not only dilute their strength in the congress, but they might actually lose some house seats from their own states. This means that so long as the Republicans have a majority in congress the possibility of Puerto Rican statehood is slim to non existent.

A second fact that has made the statehood option difficult to achieve is that the Democratic Party has been allied with the Popular Democratic Party on the island. Almost all of the delegation to the Democratic Party convention are members of the Popular Democratic Party and are therefore opposed to statehood. The official Democratic Party position has been that whatever status option the Puerto Rican people are in favor of, they will support. This is a far cry from throwing their support decisively behind the statehood option.

Another fact that has complicated the status issue is the language situation. Some senators and representatives would probably vote against statehood for Puerto Rico unsless the island were to adopt English as the only official language. Many Puerto Ricans would also oppose statehood if English were to be imposed on them in place of their native Language.

There are also some senators and representatives who may be opposed to statehood, because it would create a strong Hispanic lobby, which the believe would lead the United States towards a multicultural and multilingual state which they view as sort of a "Balkanization" of the country.

The Commonwealth status or "Estado Libre Asociado" is the present status of the island. Supporters of the present status would like to see an "enhanced commonwealth", in which the island would be granted more autonomy and would end the present colonial status. Once this process were to be completed a plebiscite could be held and if successful, the Popular Democratic Party could take their case to the congress and if approved by congress their status would become permanent. The fact which makes this impossible is that the congress claims that they cannot make a decision today that will bind the hands of a future congress. This means that a status resolution for commonwealth is impossible.

There are several facts that would make the option of independence difficult to achieve. The first factor is that in all of the status plebiscites independence has not been very successful. As Rubén Berrios points out, however. How can the Puerto Ricans vote against all of the benefits they now receive from the United States. If the United States were to guarantee the people of the island dual citizenship, as well as other benefits, this would help their status option, but this would be an unlikely possibility. These facts make it difficult to take the independence option seriously.

Nationalism is a fact that influences all of the status debate. In all of their cultural identities the Puerto Ricans are different from the predominant culture of the United States. To name only a few of these differences, we can mention language, literature, sports, music, art, etc.. The statehood advocates a kind of "Jibaro" statehood in which all of Puerto Rican cultural differences would be protected. Nationalism influences the status debate for American congressmen, because it would be difficult to contemplate the admission of Puerto Rico to the union with an organized party still in favor of independence. Nationalism of the type we find in Puerto Rico can only be understood in terms of the Civil War in the United States. General Robert E. Lee, when faced with the decision of remaining with the United States or fighting for his native state of Virginia chose the latter.

A major factor which needs to be taken into consideration by both Puerto Ricans and the congress of the United States is the population problem. The major argument that can be leveled against the independence solution is population. If Puerto Rico had a population of 500,000 people it is easy to see independence as an alternative, but with a population of roughly 3,700,000 with only slightly more than 3,300 square miles it becomes less appealing. This fact is usually not mentioned in the plebiscite campaigns. More than that is the ecological and economic argument. Unfortunately, Puerto Rico has modelled itself after that of the United States and has become a "throw away" society, a result of this has been the fact that none of the land fills on the island meet standards established on the mainland. In other words the island is choking on trash from Burger King and MacDonalds.

Victoria "Melo" Muñoz, the daughter of Luis Muñoz Marin and a former candidate for the governorship, argued that Puerto Rico should have adopted an economic model which would have been more suitable for their island environment. The enormous pharmaceutical complex on the island which has been fed by tax breaks has led to a great deal of pollution which is a much greater problem that on the mainland, given the limited size of the island.

An important argument to be considered in any discussion of Puerto Rican -v U.S. relations is the fact that the United States has served as an escape valve for the surplus population of Puerto Rico. In the beginning the United States absorbed a lot of migrant agricultural laborers and while this is still true, the emphasis today is on the migration of professionals to the mainland. Given the fact of over population, the lack of sufficient jobs and the availability of federal monies for education, it is not surprising that the Unied States is attracting a new type of migrant. The attraction would be even greater if more Puerto Ricans had taken advantage of learning English which was available to them in their schools and universities. The escape valve is one of the reasons that whatever political status should be ultimately adopted, should allow for a continuing migration to and from the mainland.

Another item which has become important in the over one hundred years of U.S., Puerto Rican relations is that we have become increasingly interdependent. This interdependence includes not only the obvious things such as the fact that we both use the U.S. Postal Service, but the fact that many people from the mainland have moved to Puerto Rico and have married with the islanders and their children are a product of both cultures. This is also true of the many Puerto Ricans who have married mainlanders and now live in Iowa or Florida. The fact is that many Puerto Ricans have served with Americans in various wars and have attended mainland universities and are active alumni members of these institutions. In addition we can mention the hundreds of thousands of Puerto Ricans who have served in the United States military forces from World War I, to Desert Storm. Some of them have risen to the very highest levels of their respective branch of them have risen to the very highest levels of their respective branch of service, such as Admiral Horacio Riveró and Air Force General Salvodor Felices. Many Puerto Rican ex-servicemen are members of the V.F.W or the American Legion, etc., and have active ties with their comrades on the mainland. We could also mention the ties between fraternal organizations such as the Rotary Club, the Elks Club - or the Lions' Club to mention just a few.

Imagine a Puerto Rican living in Ponce, who stops on his way to work to have breakfast at Dennys and then goes on to his job at K Mart. After work he picks up his wife who is working as an assistant manager at Walgreens. They stop to buy a tire for their Ford at Sears and then they run home to have some Kentucky Fried Chicken, after which the husband goes to his Rotary Club Meeting, while his wife watches Monica Lewinsky being interviewed by Barbara Walters on TV.

The inderdependence between Puerto Rico and the United States has developed for over a hundred years and any change in the status quo will prove to be very difficult.

The original proposition of this chapter was to determine whether certain facts or realities were present which would lead us to a possible solution to the status situation. Even if, in some future plebiscite the statehood option were to obtain 51% of the vote, opponents would argue that in order to grant statehood we need a larger majority in order to seriously consider Puerto Rico for admission into the union.

The Commonwealth option has been, and is, a viable alternative, but members of congress have said that they could not make permanent an enhanced Commonwealth for the island, because they cannot make a decision that binds a future congress that might want to approve statehood, independence, or some other option for the island.

Advocates of Commonwealth status are then in a no win situation, because every few years a new plebiscite can be held until finally the people will simply throw up their hands and select a less desired alternative.

Independence, or the type of independence favored by its leaders, would seem to be an elusive possibility. Most Puerto Ricans are sympathetic towards the idea of independence, but they also are afraid of that option. Rubén Berrios, the leader of the independence movement would like to see a dual citizenship for Puerto Ricans and to have a period of say 10 years during which time Puerto Rico would continue to receive money from the federal government, etc. If Puerto Rico were to receive what the independence leaders would like from the United States, there is a possibility that the independence option would be more attractive to the voters, but be the reality is that for the moment, the independence option is not a viable one.

This leaves us with another possibility, that of Free Association or a "bilateral compact" between the United States and Puerto Rico. At first glance, this option would appear to be preposterous, but at second glance it would appear to make some sense. In the first place, there are too many obstacles in the path of statehood and the congress has to make it clear that the commonwealth status cannot become permanent, therefore, it is doomed to come to an end at some future date. Independence, probably the emotional favorite of a majority of the population is doomed to failure, because of the economic and demographic consequences.

Free Association on the other hand has a number of advantages. The main idea of Free Association is the contract between two sovereign nations. The concept here is that negotiations would take place between the United

States and Puerto Rico and once the negotiations would be completed to the satisfaction of both parties, Puerto Rico would be granted their independence and then immediately afterwards a treaty would go into effect which would spell out the details of the "bilateral compact".

Puerto Rico would "probably" receive most of what they want, they would no longer be a colony and they would have entered into the "bilateral compact" of their own free will. Their Olympic team and beauty pageants and their language would be protected as a result of the negotiations. The negotiations would also provide a transition period during which time federal funds would continue to be received by the island, but possibly at a reduced rate. Dual citizenship could also be chip at the negotiation table, because of the "bilateral compact", whereas it would probably not be granted to a completely independent Puerto Rico.

The question which the critics of this idea might raise at this point is: "What's in it for the United States"? There are several reasons why the United States might go along with Free Association. The first reason is that Puerto Rico is a major customer for American exports and Free Association would have the effect of continuing this situation. A more important reason in the opinion of some is the strategic importance of Puerto Rico. There are those who believe that Puerto Rico is still of vital importance in the defense fo the nation. On "April 5, 1989, former senator James McClure, R-Idaho mentioned strategic denial and base rights as two, crucial interests of the United States with all three parties"./173 Juan M. García Passalacgua, the well known political observer and commentator, who is in favor of the "bilateral compact" agues that in exchange for the use of various military installations on the island, "the present level of federal funding should be frozen in a block grant for and extensive period of years"./174 In other words the United States would be willing to agree to Free Association in exchange for the economic advantages which it presently enjoys and its military bases.

The solution proposed in the conclusion appears to be rather drastic, but it fits the facts as we know them. We have seen that the development of a strong nationalistic feeling is hostile to the statehood idea. We have also seen that the independence option has never galvanized the voters in any of the various plebiscites which have been promulgated over the years. The other possibility, which has a great deal of support among the people is the commonwealth status option. The Commonwealth supporters want what they refer to as a culmination of Commonwealth, which when approved by congress and the Puerto Rican people would be a permanent solution. The congress of the United States has taken the position that a permanent commonwealth cannot be established, because the congress does not have the right to bind the hands of some future congress that might want to grant independence or statehood to the island.

The advantage of the Free Association option is the fact that the United States would most likely be able to retain control of their military bases, which it considers to be absolutely necessary for strategic reasons. Puerto Rico would most likely be able to retain many of the advantages which they presently enjoy under the Commonwealth status. The main advantage is the fact that a negotiated agreement would end the endless status debate as well as a lot of hypocrisy. The end of the status debate and the establishment of free association would lead to a more harmonious relationship based on shared ideals and goals for the future.

FOOTNOTES

1. "Letter from Congress to the People of Puerto Rico" February 29, 1996, <u>San Juan Star,</u> April 14, 1996, pp 6, 7.
2. lbid.
3. lbid.
4. lbid.
5. lbid.
6. lbid.
7. "Elections in Puerto Rico" File: /1/A/Elections Net, htm, Source: Manuel Alvarez- Rivera. 03/06/97 16:27.21 pp. 1 & 2
8. "Descifrando el mensaje de las elecciones Sobre la Independencia de Puerto Rico" Latinolink: Descifrando...Pendencia de Puerto Rico File///A\ /elections\.net. Htm. Source: Lance Oliver 03/06/97, 16:22:52, pp. 1-3
9. lbid.
10. lbid.
11. lbid.
12. Robert Friedman, "Commonwealth at 40: Old Age or Midlife?" <u>San Juan Star</u>. July 26, 1992.
13. lbid.
14. Francisco A. Scarano, Puerto Rico: <u>Cinco Siglos de Historia,</u> Santa Fé de Bogota, Columbia: McGraw-Hill Interamericana, S.A. 1993, p. 677.,
15. lbid. p. 683.
16. Fernando Picó <u>Historia General de Puerto Rico: Rio Piedras,</u> Puerto Rico: Ediciones huraca_. 1988, p. 260
17. lbid. p. 270
18. lbid. p. 278

19. Robert Friedman, "The Young Bill: A Special Report." San Juan Star, April 13, 1997, p. 3

20. Alex W. Maldonado, "Where is the Puerto Rico Going? San Juan Star, July 14, 1988.

21. Leonor Mulero, "Tougher Regulations on Financial Aid" El Nuevo Dia, January, 1993.

22. Ibid.

23. Alex W. Maldonado, "Saga of a Tuition Increase" San Juan Star, May 10, 1992.

24. Ibid.

25. Robert Friedman, "Puerto Rican Students Eligible for Service Programs" San Juan Star, March 6, 1993.

26. Ibid.

27. "Annual Report", Inter American University of Puerto Rico, Ponce Campus, June 1992.

28. Douglas Zehr, "Survey: Men want Olympic Team" San Juan Star, October 7, 1993.

29. A. W. Maldonado, "Olympic Hopes of NPP Reflects a Larger Issue" San Juan Star, October 7, 1993.

30. María Bird Picó, "All Parties Stroke the National Identity - Nationalism," San Juan Star, September 26, 1993.

31. Ibid.

32. Javier Maymi, "Puerto Rico Faces Olympic Identity Crisis" San Juan Star, August 3, 1993.

33. Ibid.

34. Ibid.

35. Benny Frankie Cerezo, Plebescite Campaign Flawed Cultures" San Juan Star, October 3, 1993.

36. A. W. Maldonado, "A Nationhood Argument" San Juan Star, March 14, 1991.

37. Ibid.

38. Ibid.

39. A. W. Maldonado. "Language" San Juan Star, March 14, 1991.

40. A. W. Maldonado, "Lost-in-America" <u>San Juan Star</u>, June 28, 1992.

41. Victor González Ortiz, "Language" <u>El Vocero</u>, September 16, 1991.

42. Robert Friedman, "Language" <u>San Juan Star</u>, September 29, 1992.

43. Editorial, "Johnston Rips Spanish-Only" <u>San Juan Star</u>, March 9, 1991.

44. Melinda Karle, "Language" <u>San Juan Star</u>, June 22, 1991.

45. lbid.

46. Robert Glass, "Language" Associated Press, <u>San Juan Star</u>, October 13, 1991.

47. lbid.

48. lbid.

49. Glynn C. Moran, "Language" Reader's Viewpoint, <u>San Juan Star</u>, October 6, 1992.

50. lbid.

51. Editorial, "The Language Prize", <u>San Juan Star</u>, October 17, 1991.

52. lbid.

53. Bennie Frankie Cerezo, "Plebiscite Campaign Flawed" <u>San Juan Star</u>, October 3, 1993.

54. Robert Friedman, "The Young Bill: A Special Report" <u>San Juan Star</u>, April 13, 1997. p. 4

55. lbid. p. 4

56. Robert Friedman, "Language, Citizenship to the forefront: The Young Bill: A special Report" <u>San Juan Star</u>, April 13, 199. p.5.

57. lbid, p. 5.

58. Tom Bryan, "Caribbean Business Week" August 13, 1992.

59. Elsa Tío, "Descolonización y Lenguaje" Perspectiva. <u>El Nuevo Dia</u>, May 9 1997, p. 79.

60. Carmen Millan Pabón, "Advertencia de Guerra a los

Maestros de EE. U. U." El Nuevo Dia, May 16, 1997. p. 21.

61. "Fufi" Santori, "Pollito-chicken", Perspectiva, El Nuevo Dia, May 10, 1997, p. 89.

62. Robert Friedman, "P. R. to gain in food funds despite Pan Cuts". San Juan Star, January 19, 1995, p. 3.

63. Tom Bryan, "Caribbean Business Week, August 13, 1992.

64. Robert Friedman, "P. R. to gain in food funds despite Pan Cuts". San Juan Star, January 19, 1995, p. 3.

65. lbid, p. 3.

66. Robert Friedman, "No Insular Jurisdictions pay Federal Taxes". San Juan Star, February 12, 1995, p. 6.

67. lbid, p. 6.

68. lbid, p. 6.

69. Jorge Medina, "Section 936 Faces changes in the Decade" San Juan Star, September 7, 1992.

70. lbid.

71. Leonor Mulero, "Bonanza, More Money for each status option," El Nuevo Dia, October 17, 1993.

72. Robert Friedman, "No Insular Jurisdictions pay Federal Taxes". San Juan Star, February 12, 1995, p. 6.

73. A. W. Maldonado, "Lost-in-America" San Juan Star, June 28, 1992.

74. lbid.

75. lbid.

76. lbid.

77. Lawrence Barrett, "State of Anticipation" Time Magazine, November , 1993.

78. Lorraine Blasor, "Island Poll: 78% not informed on Young Bill," San Juan Star, May 15, 1997.

79. Harry Turner, "Congress urged to Eliminate 936" San Juan Star, May 15, 1992.
80. Ibid.
81. Ibid.
82. Ibid.
83. Jorge Medina, "Section 936 Faces change" San Juan Star, September 7, 1992.
84. Ibid.
85. A. W. Maldonado, "Economics and Language", San Juan Star, May 5, 1991.
86. Jorge Medina, "Section 936 Faces change" San Juan Star, September 7, 1992.
87. Doreen Hemlock, "936 Reviews not Rave in Bestseller" San Juan Star, September 10, 1992.
88. Ibid.
89. Ibid.
90. Robert Friedman "Commonwealth at 40" San Juan Star, July 26, 1992.
91. Ibid.
92. Ibid.
93. Harry Turner, "Congress urged to Eliminate 936" San Juan Star, May 15, 1992.
94. Congressional Record entry 5 of 269, "Wage - Based Tax Credit needed to stimulate job creation in Puerto Rico" House of Representatives, Page: H5304, May 21, 1996.
95. Ibid.
96. Ibid.
97. Alexander Odishelidze, Ed., "Puerto Rico at the Crossroads" The Money Mastery Newsletter, Vol. II, Issue 3, 1995, p. 7.
98. Harry Turner, "Muñoz tells Reporters in D. C., Puerto Rico not always trustworthy" San Juan Star, July 30, 1992.
99. Robert Friedman, "Runaway Existence Undesirable

says Study" <u>San Juan Star</u>, June 11, 1993.

100. Ibid.

101. Ibid.

102. Ibid.

103. Jorge Medina, "Section 936 Faces change in this Decade" <u>San Juan Star,</u> September 7, 1992.

104. Harry Turner, "Union Seeks to Halt Mainland Plants Flight to Island" <u>San Juan Star</u>, November 24, 1990

105. Harry Turner, "Section 936 said Affecting Mainland Industrial Growth" <u>San Juan Star</u>, March 31, 1988.

106. Ibid.

107. Barbara LeBlanc, "Business Today" <u>San Juan Star,</u> June 13, 1991.

108. A. W. Maldonado, "Runaway Industries", <u>San Juan Star,</u> January 14, 1993.

109. Robert Friedman, "Federal Tax Brouhaha seen Igniting a Status Firestorm" <u>San Juan Star</u>, February 12, 1995.

110. Robert Friedman, "Commonwealth at 40" <u>San Juan Star</u>, July 26, 1992.

111. Robert Friedman, "The Young Bill: A Special Report" <u>San Juan Star</u>, April 12, 1997.

112. María T. Padilla, "Bless the American Dollar" <u>Business Notebook, Puerto Rico and the IMF,</u> April 29, 1997.

113. "Hugo" <u>San Juan Star,</u> September 30, 1990.

114. Ibid.

115. Ibid.

116. Ibid.

117. Ibid.

118. Ibid.

119. Editorial, "U. S. Excise Taxes and P. R. Status" <u>San Juan Star,</u> October 14, 1992.

120. Jorge Luis Medina "P. R. will be included in the Administrations National Health Reform Plan" <u>San Juan Star,</u> June 19, 1993.

121. Ibid.

122. Robert Friedman, "Puerto Rico avoids the Cigarette Tax for Health Plan," <u>San Juan Star,</u> October 2, 1993.

123. Leonor Mulero, "Tougher Regulations on Educational Aid," <u>El Nuevo Dia,</u> January 24, 1994.

124. Carl and Jessica Bridenbaugh, <u>Rebels and Gentlemen: Philadelphia in the Age of Franklin,</u> A Heperides Book, New York

125. Karl Ross, "PIP Greets Gutiérrez with Hero's Welcome" <u>San Juan Star,</u> December 1, 1992.

126. Ibid.

127. Ibid.

128. Robert Friedman, "Amnesty says Macheteros not Common Criminals," <u>San Juan Star,</u> December 1, 1992.

129. María Bird Picó, "Post Plebiscite Anxiety Rejection is Found Collective Fear of U. S. Rejection" <u>San Juan Star,</u> September 26, 1993.

130. María Bird Picó, "All Parties Stroke National Identity Nationalism" <u>San Juan Star,</u> September 26, 1993.

131. A. W. Maldonado, "A Nationhood Argument", <u>San Juan Star,</u> March 24, 1991.

132. Julio Ghigliotty, "U. S. Certifies Mari Bras' Loss of Nationality" <u>San Juan Star,</u> December 5, 1995.

133. Ibid.

134. Ibid.

135. Ibid.

136. Ibid.

137. Editorial, <u>San Juan Star,</u> October 23, 1966.

138. Ibid.

139.Melba Ferrer, "Two Nations? One Vote," <u>San Juan Star,</u> October 23, 1966.

140.Juan M. García Passalacqua, "Time has Come to Cash in Military Bargaining Chip" <u>San Juan Star,</u> January 15, 1995.

141.Robert Friedman, "Lott Cities P.R. Indecision in Delay of Bill", <u>The San Juan Star,</u> September 17, 1998.

142."C.R.B.: Republicans Fear Democratic P.R. <u>The San Juan Star,</u> September 13, 1998.

143.Enrique Vásquez Quíntana, <u>La Gran Decepción,</u> Produción por Editorial Macaná, San Juan, Puerto Rico: 1996, pp. 201-207.

144.Angel Rivero, <u>Crónica de la Guerra Hispano Americano en Puerto Rico,</u> Plus Ultra, Educational Publishers, Inc. New York: 1973, pp. 25-36.

145.Ibid, pp. 25-32.

146.Ibid, pp. 25-32.

147.Enríque Vásquez Quíntana, <u>La Gran Decepción,</u> Productión por Editorial Macaná, San Juan, Puerto Rico: 1996, Inc. p. 203.

148.Ibid., p. 204.

149.Francisco A. Scarano, <u>Cinco Siglos de Historia,</u> McGraw Hill, San Juan, Puerto Rico, 1993, p. 753.

150.Ibid, p. 754.

151.Ibid, p. 763.

152.Mark Kurlansky, <u>A Continent of Islands: Searching for the Caribbean Destiny,</u> Addison Wesley Publishing Co., New York: 1992, p. 242

153.Ibid, p. 242.

154.Ibid, pp. 242-243.

155.Enríque Vásquez Quíntana, <u>La Gran Decepción,</u> Productión por Editorial Macaná, San Juan, Puerto Rico: 1996, Inc. p. 66.

156.Ibid, p. 67.

157. Ibid, p. 68.
158. John Marino, "None of the Above Wins", <u>The San Juan Star,</u> December 14, 1998. p. 5.
159. Ibid, p. 5.
160. Ibid, p. 6.
161. Eva Llorens Vélez, "No. 5 Prevails in Spite of PDP Division, lack of funds", <u>The San Juan Star,</u> December 14, 1998. p. 5.
162. Rafael F. Franco, "Berrios: Voters have killed Commonwealth Status", <u>The San Juan Star,</u> December 14, 1998. p. 9.
163. Proviana Colon Díaz, "Vega Ramos: ProELA wins in long run", <u>The San Juan Star,</u> December 14, 1998. p. 9.
164. Ibid, p. 9.
165. Robert Friedman, "Whitehouse to Rush for another Plebiscite", <u>The San Juan Star,</u> p. 5.
166. Ibid, p. 5.
167. Ibid, p. 5.
168. Ibid, p. 5.
169. Frank Ramos, "The Meaning of the Status Plebiscite Results", <u>The San Juan Star,</u> December 18, 1998. p. 57.
170. Ibid, p. 57.
171. Ibid, p. 57.
172. Marty Garard Delfín, "Rosselló: 5th Colunm Win was a Protest Vote", <u>The San Juan Star,</u> December 14, 1998. p. 7.
173. Juan M. García Passalacqua, "Time has come to Cash in Military Bargaining Chip" <u>The San Juan Star,</u> January 15, 1995.
174. Ibid.

ABOUT THE AUTHOR

An Air Force veteran of the Korean War, Professor Irving studied at UCLA, the University of Connecticut, Wesleyan University and U.S.I.U. He worked as an instructor and administrator at the Univ. of Connecticut and is presently working as an adjunct professor at Eastern New Mexico University, in Roswell, New Mexico. For 27 years of his professional career he worked in Puerto Rico as an Associate Prof. of History and as an administrator for the Inter American University of P.R. for 14 years, he taught, among other courses, the History of Puerto Rico in Spanish.